FLOWERS OF FANTASY

A Coloring Book of
Fantastical Flower Designs, Flowers in Vases, Flowers and Poetry and More!

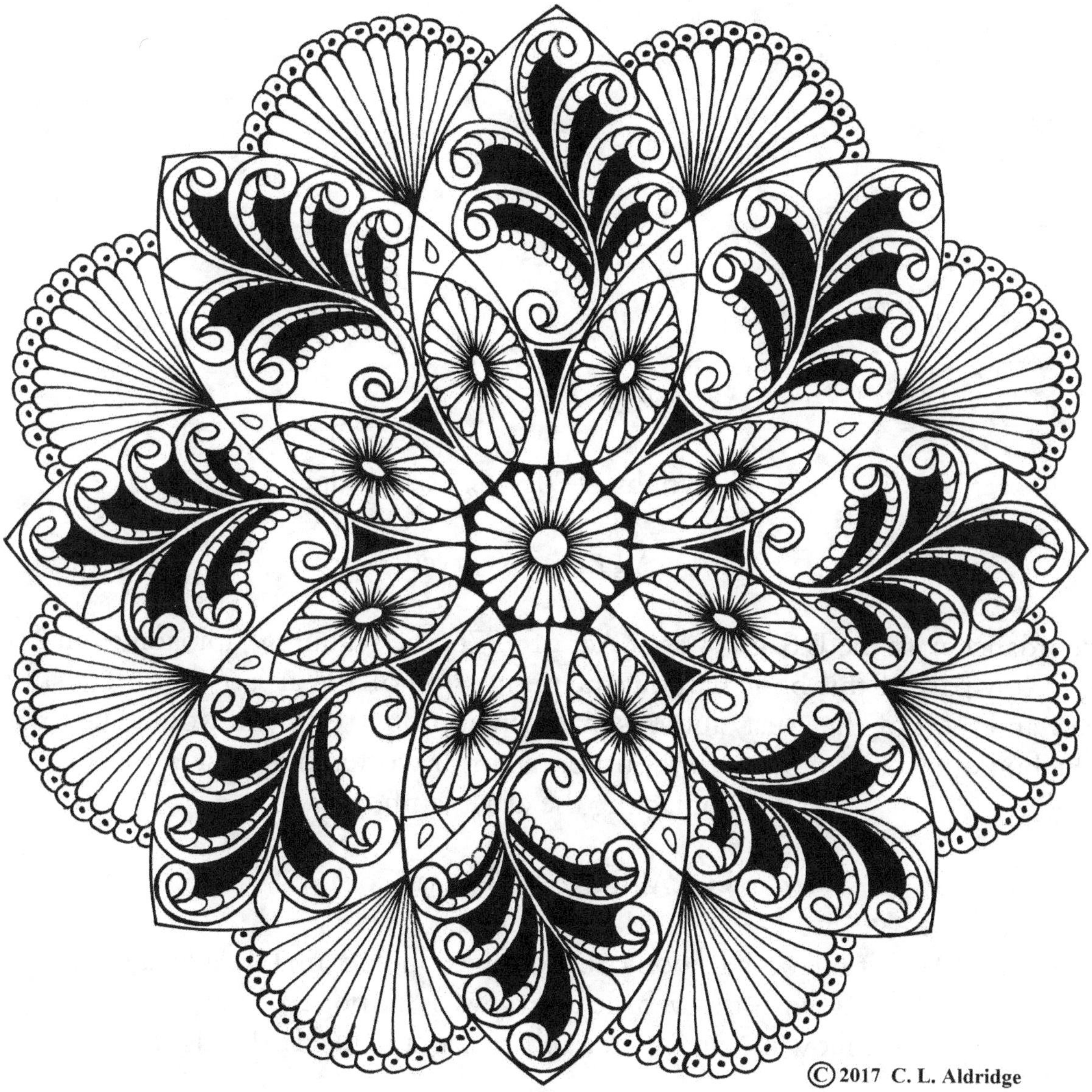

© 2017 C. L. Aldridge

Illustrations by: C. L. Aldridge

ISBN-13:978-1547035731
ISBN-10:1547035730

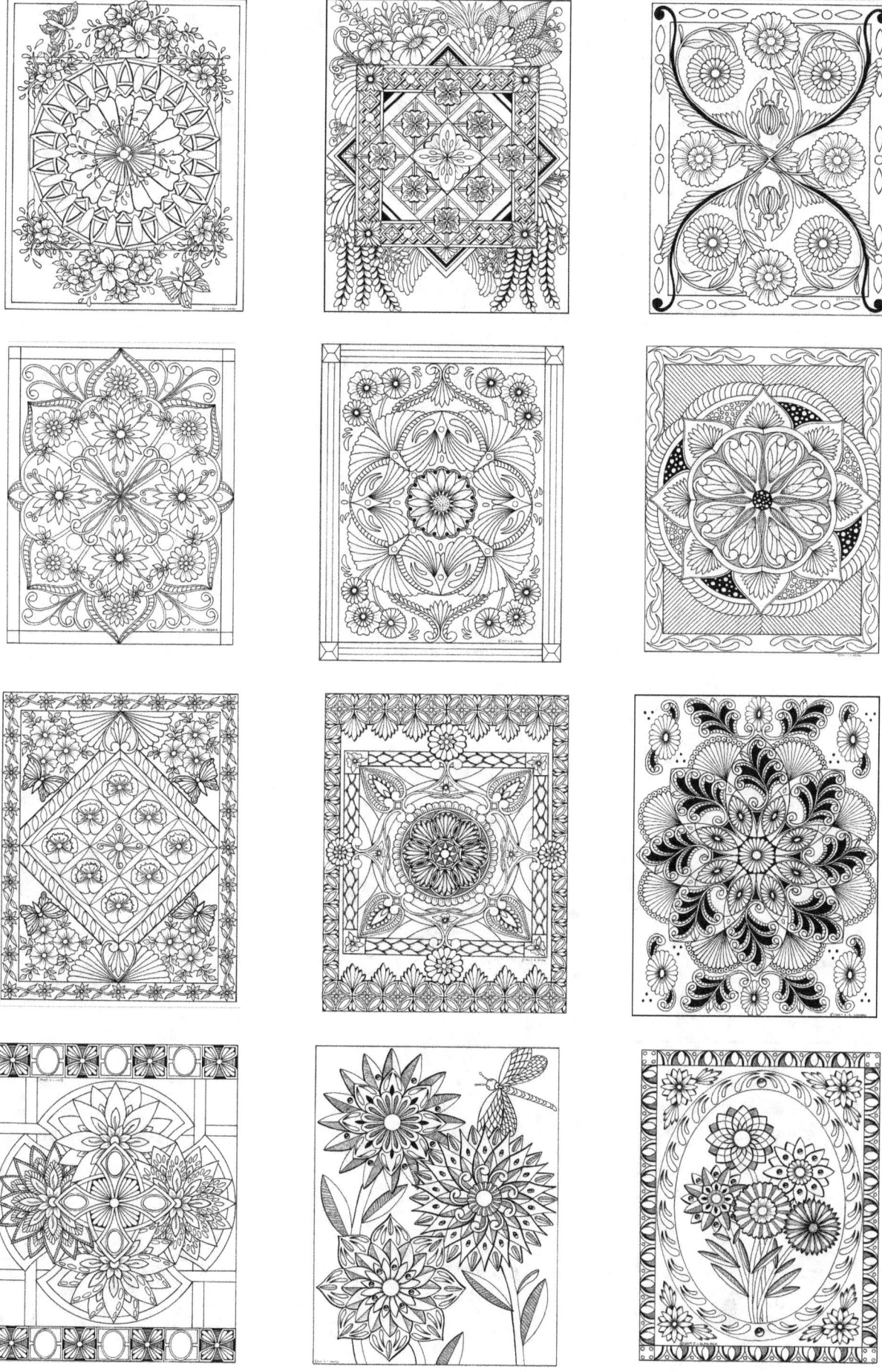

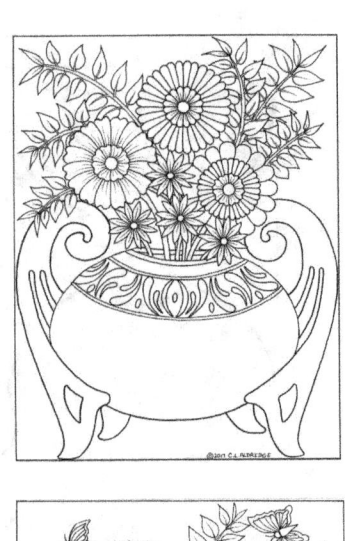
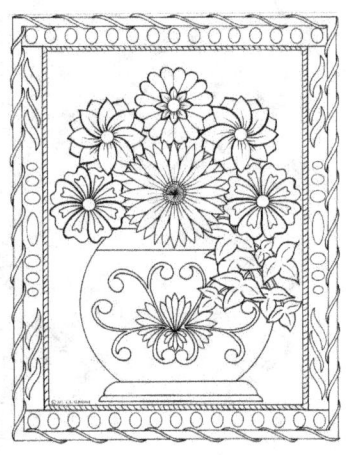
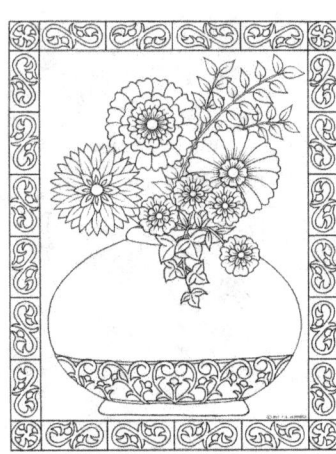
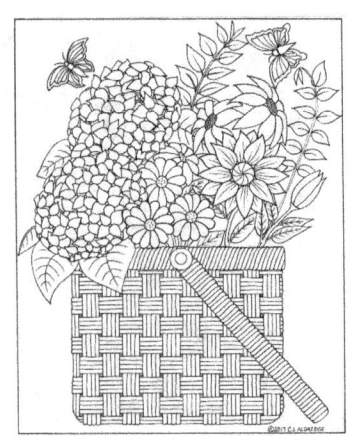
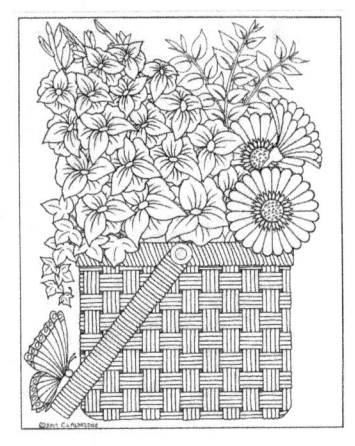
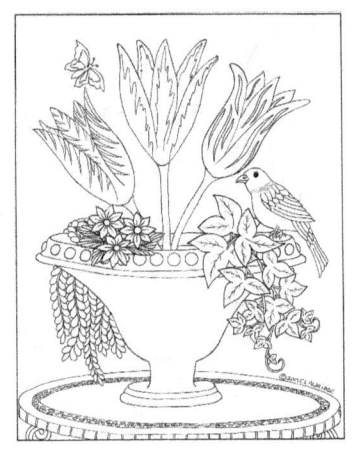
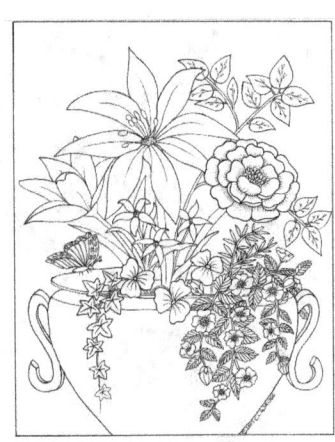
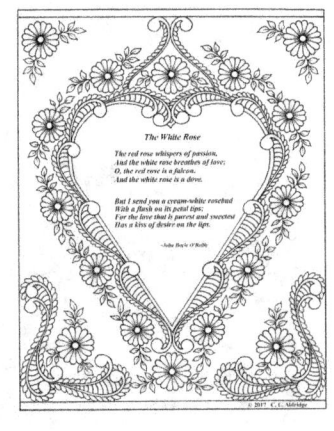
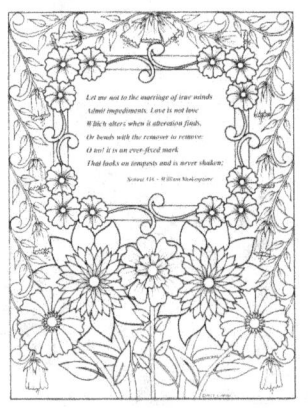
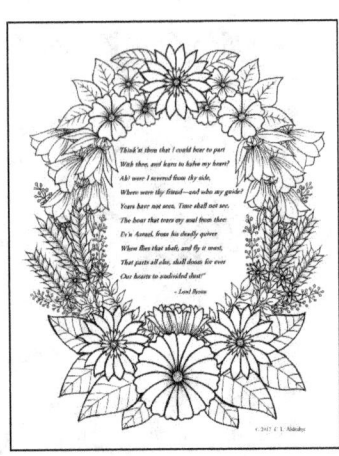
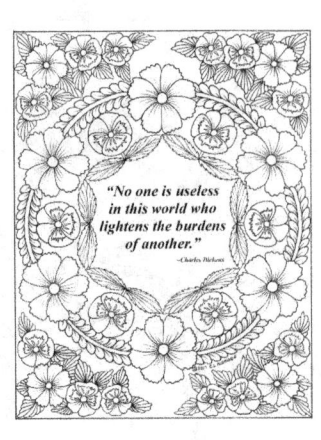
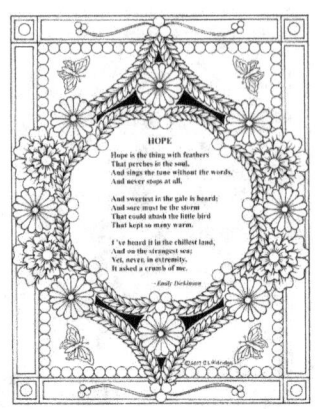

PLUS A FULL SET OF 24 - CRAFT/GREETING CARD SIZE,
Printed 2 per page— sample layouts below

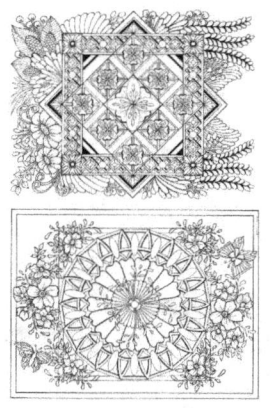 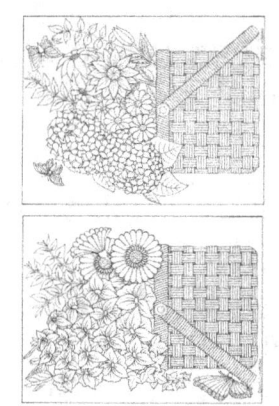 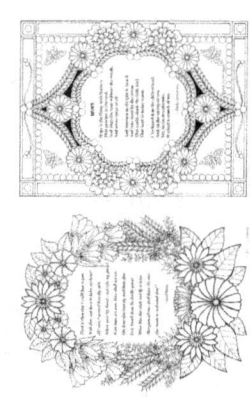

PLUS 6 BONUS PAGES!

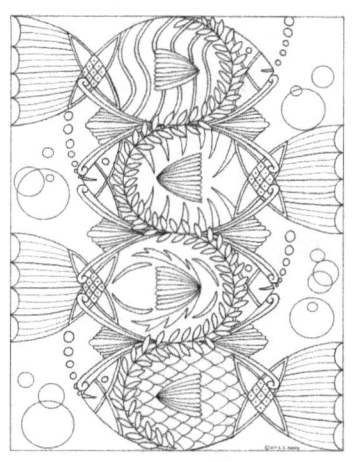 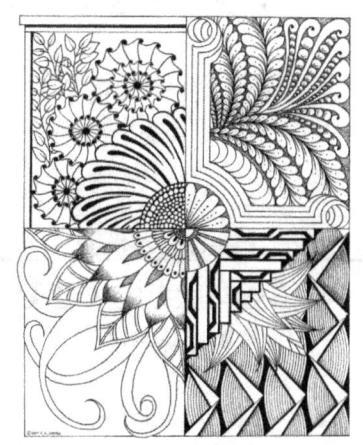 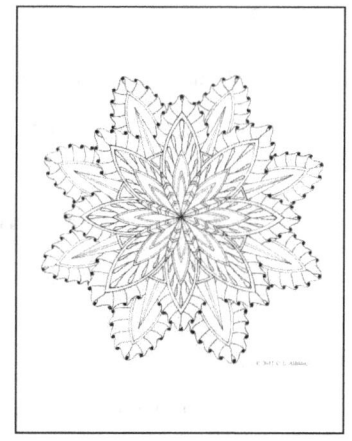

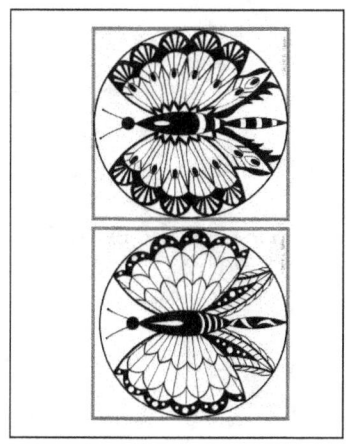 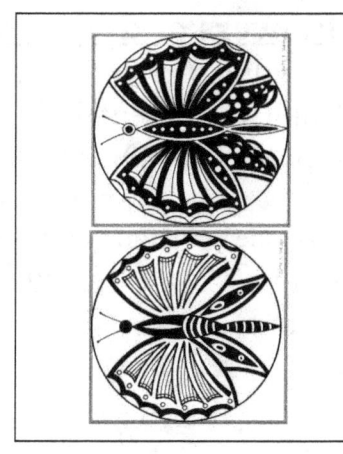 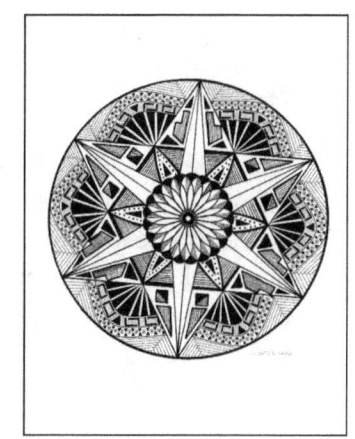

Also by C. L. Aldridge

Flowers and Dreams
A Coloring Book of Beautiful Botanical Symmetry

- This book is so elegant that when you finish coloring it you want to frame every one! - Jun. 16, 2016 ~ *Amazon Customer* (now in it's 2nd Edition), first pub. Jan. 7, 2016

Adult Coloring Book of Flower Inspirations
Beautiful Floral Patterns, Botanical Mandalas, Gemstones, Lovely Words and More!

- C. L. Aldridge has hit it out of the ballpark again! Just as with her first book, "Flowers and Dreams," this one is filled with the most unique and gorgeous floral coloring pages you'll find. Her pages are designed with consideration for any medium you choose to use. I'll be anxiously awaiting the release of a third book! - June 10, 2016 ~ *E. Siegel* (pub. April 24, 2016)

Flowers and Flyers
Adult Coloring Book of Flowers, Songbirds, Hummingbirds, Butterflies, Owls, Ornamentals and More!

- I have all 3 of C L Aldridge's books. I own lots of adult coloring books. These 3 are at the top of my list! - Sept. 30, 2016 ~ *C. Ames* (published Aug. 24, 2016)

Travel Size Book of Flowers, Birds Butterflies and More!
Your Coloring Book for the Road.

- Measures 6" x 9", just the right size to tuck in a purse, a travel bag or a desk drawer. (Pub. Sept. 23, 2016). Features 36 drawings… 12 from each of the Artists first 3 books above.

Flowers and Whimsy
Adult Coloring Book of Fun to Color Ornamental Floral Patterns, Whimsical Butterflies, Dragonflies and More!

- Drop dead gorgeous drawings, one after another. Every page is a feast for the eyes. All of her books are glorious. –April 28, 2017 ~ *J. Fanning* (published Dec. 3, 2016)

This book is dedicated to the fans at:
C. L. Aldridge's, Coloring in Bloom-Coloring Club
on Facebook, whose faith in my Art, and whose daily encouragement,
brings such joy to my life. Also to my dear friend and fellow artist
Susan Curry, for her enthusiasm and support!

A very special thank you to colorists: Virginia Sanders Cole,
Susan Curry, and Elizabeth Zack Siegel for so generously
allowing me to use their colored renderings of my drawings
on the cover of this book.

* * * *

IMPORTANT INFORMATION FOR USING THIS BOOK

- This book contains 48 hand-drawn illustrations to color, each is printed SINGLE SIDED (back is blank). Plus 6 additional bonus pages!

- Illustrations are printed in TWO SIZES, a full size page and a crafters size (suitable for a 5" x 7" frame, mounting to a greeting card face or scrapbook page, etc). Please note the crafters sizes are also single sided and are printed two on a page.

- The pages are printed on #60 lb bright white paper which performs well for all brands of colored pencils and crayons, without the need of a blotter page.

- To avoid any "Uh Oh's" and the associated disappointment, **Marker and Gel Pen users are STRONGLY ENCOURAGED to USE A BLOTTER SHEET** behind the drawing to avoid any possibility of bleed through to the next page. Several blank blotter and color testing pages are provided at the end of this book.

- Most IMPORTANT of all: Relax, have fun, stand-up and stretch often, and remember that sometimes the most beautiful things come from what we think at first are mistakes, but which turn out to be art's way of working magic!

This Book Belongs To:

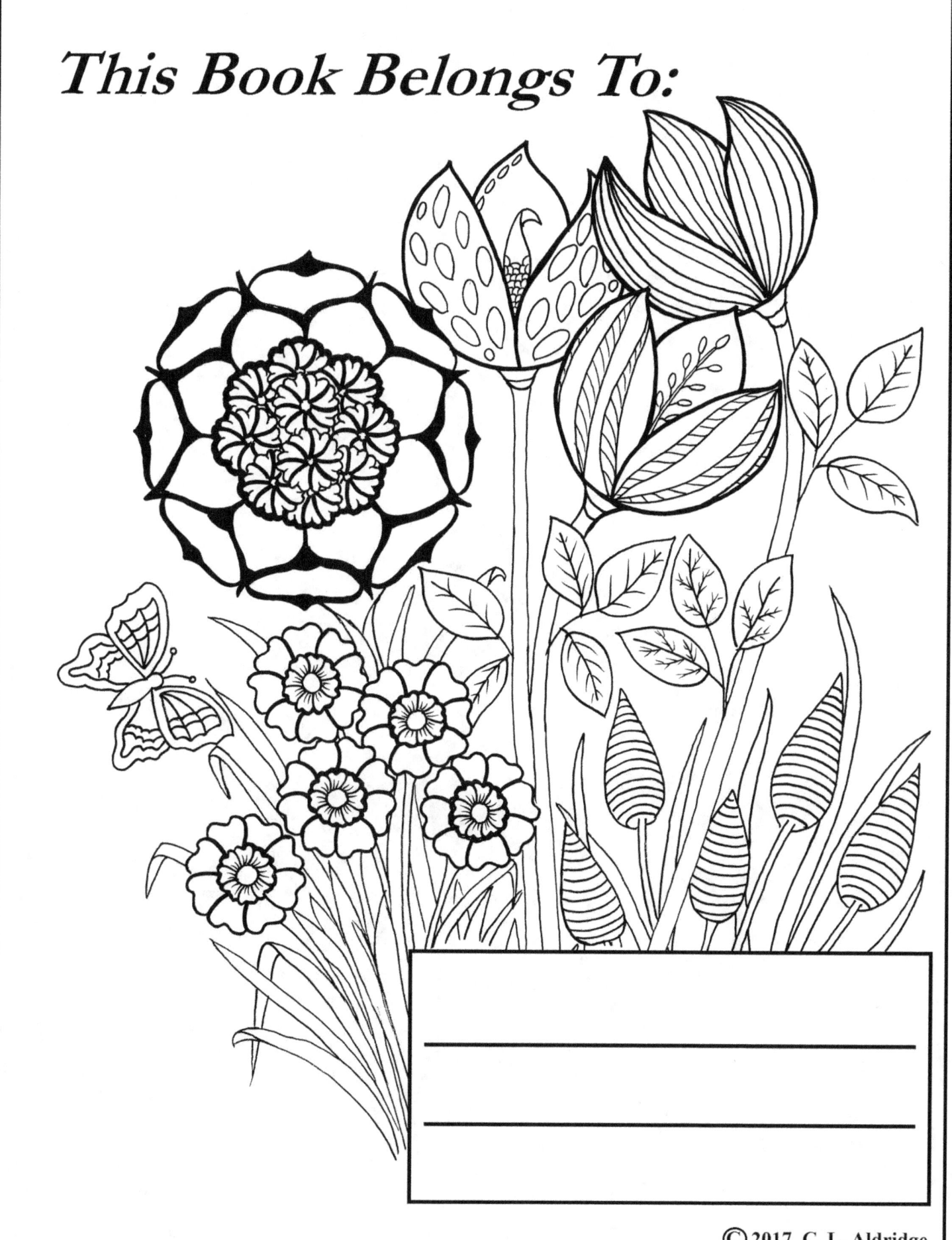

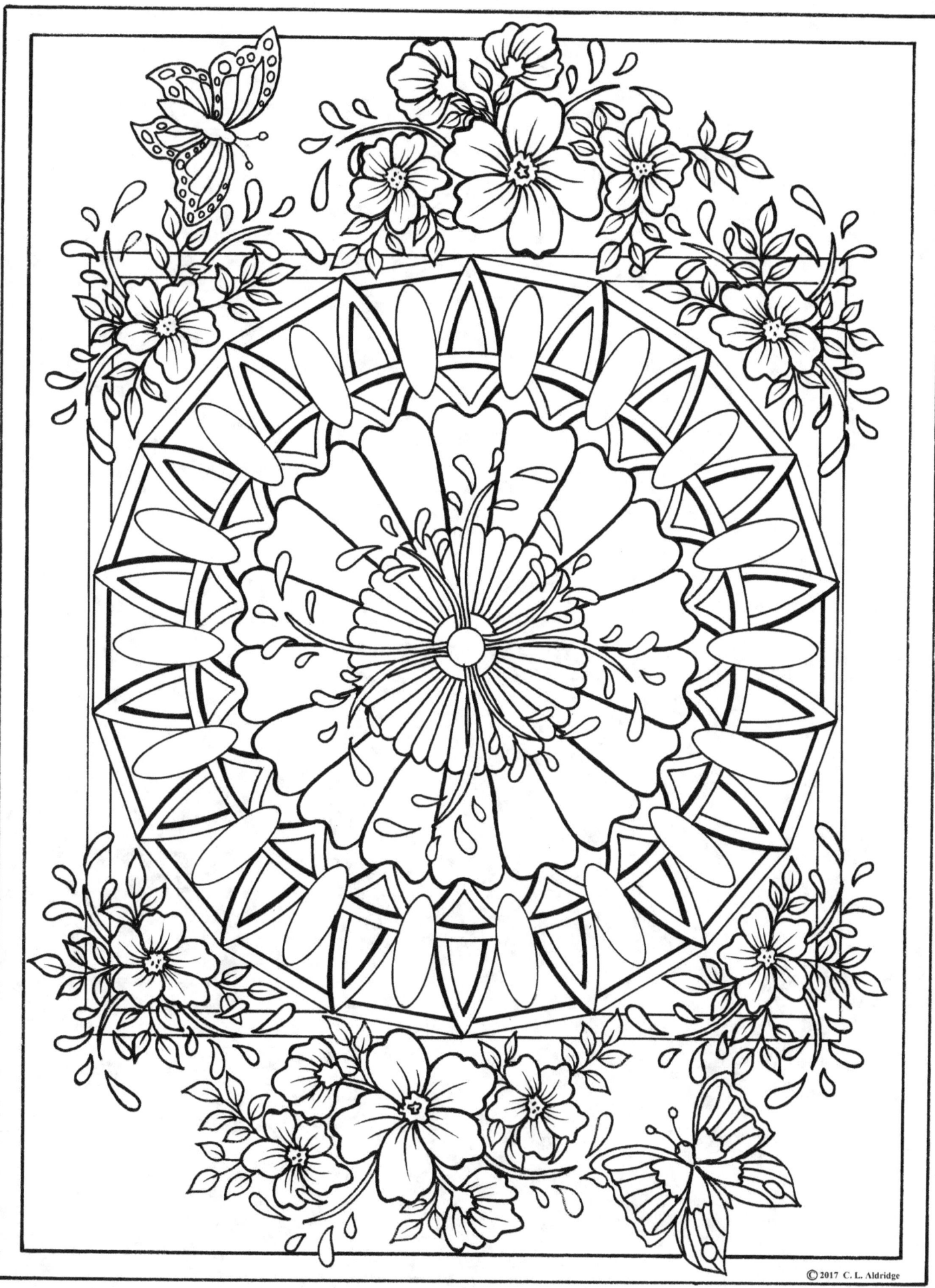

© 2017 C. L. Aldridge

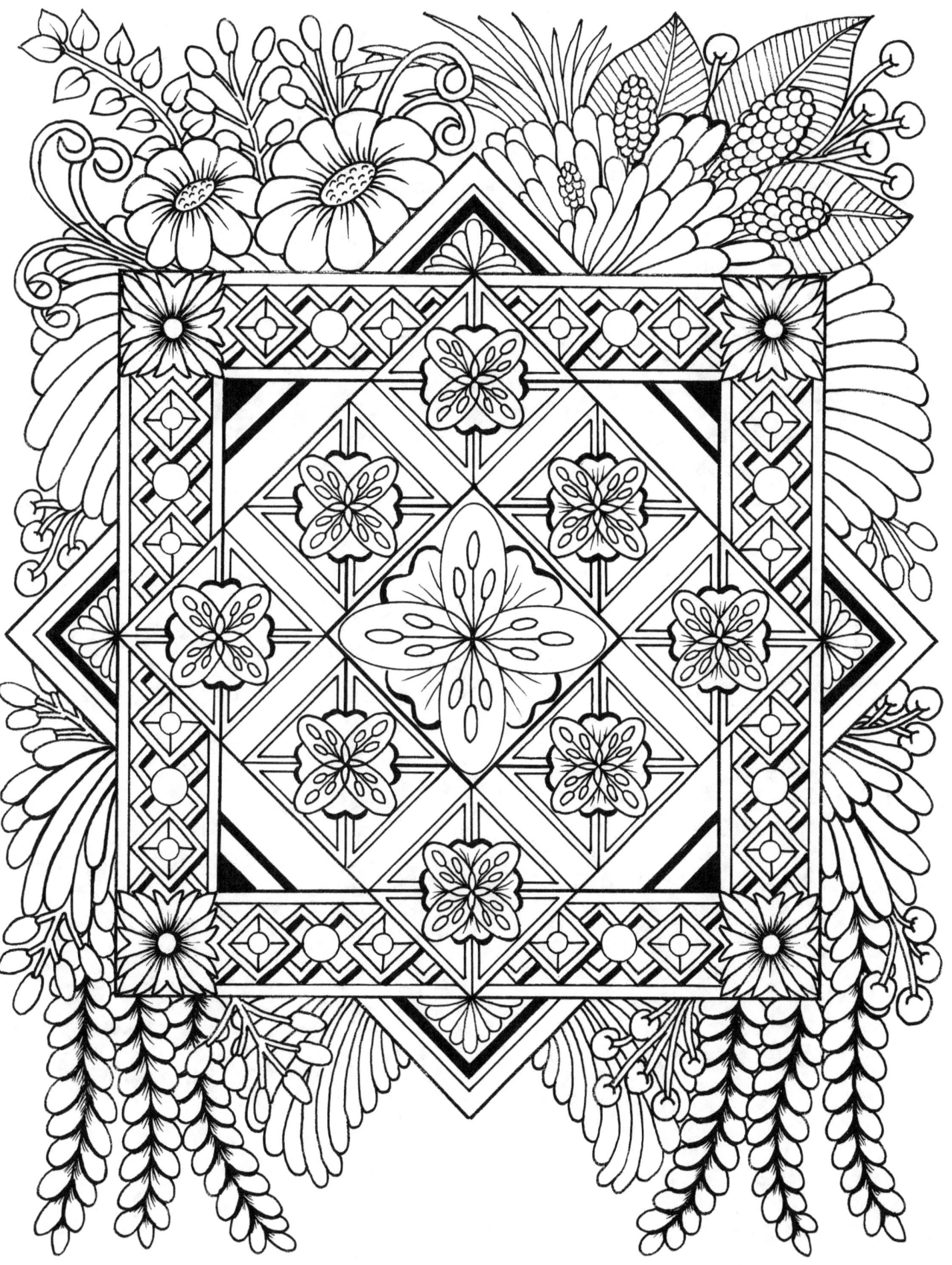

© 2017 C. L. Aldridge

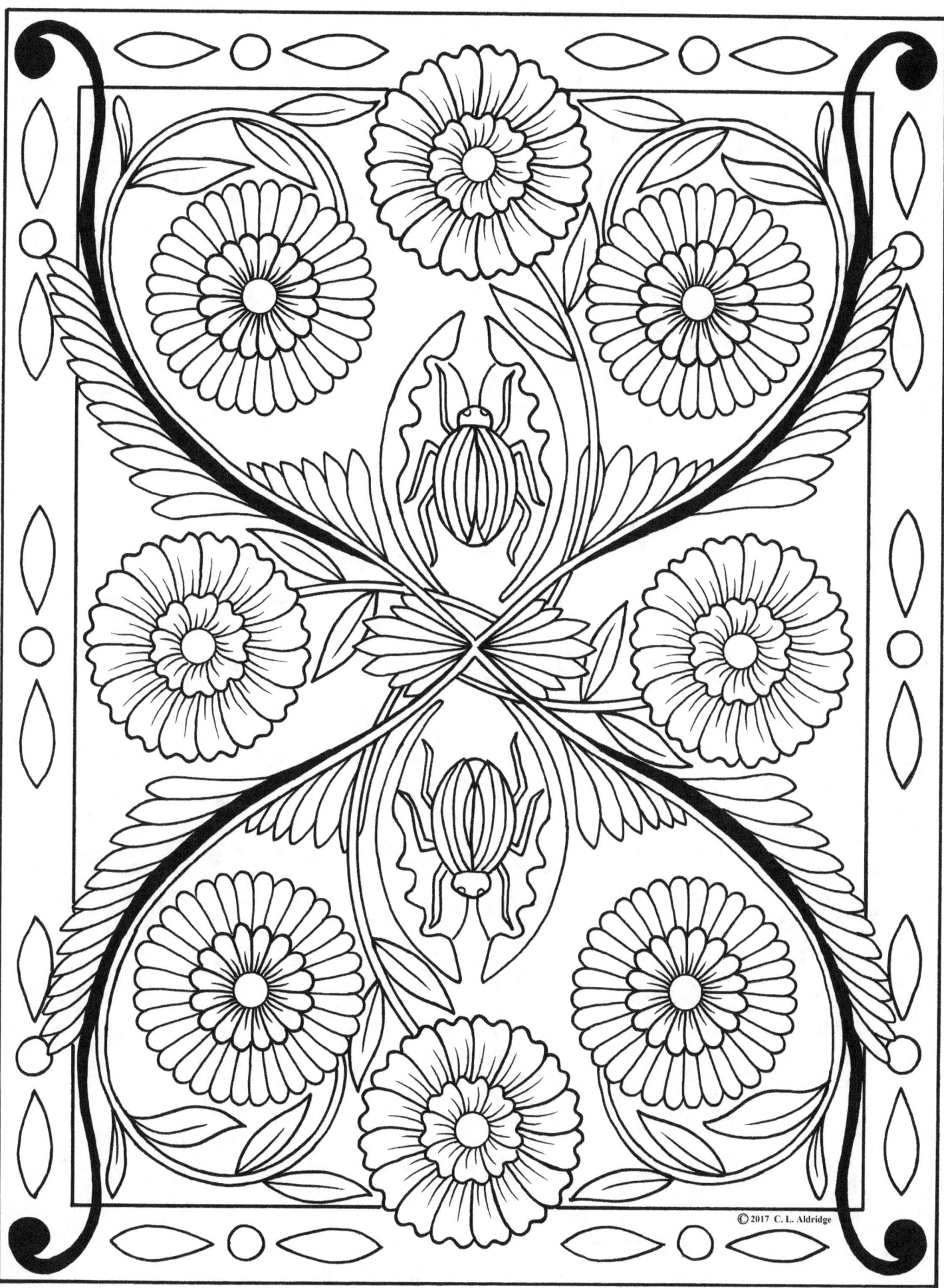

© 2017 C. L. Aldridge

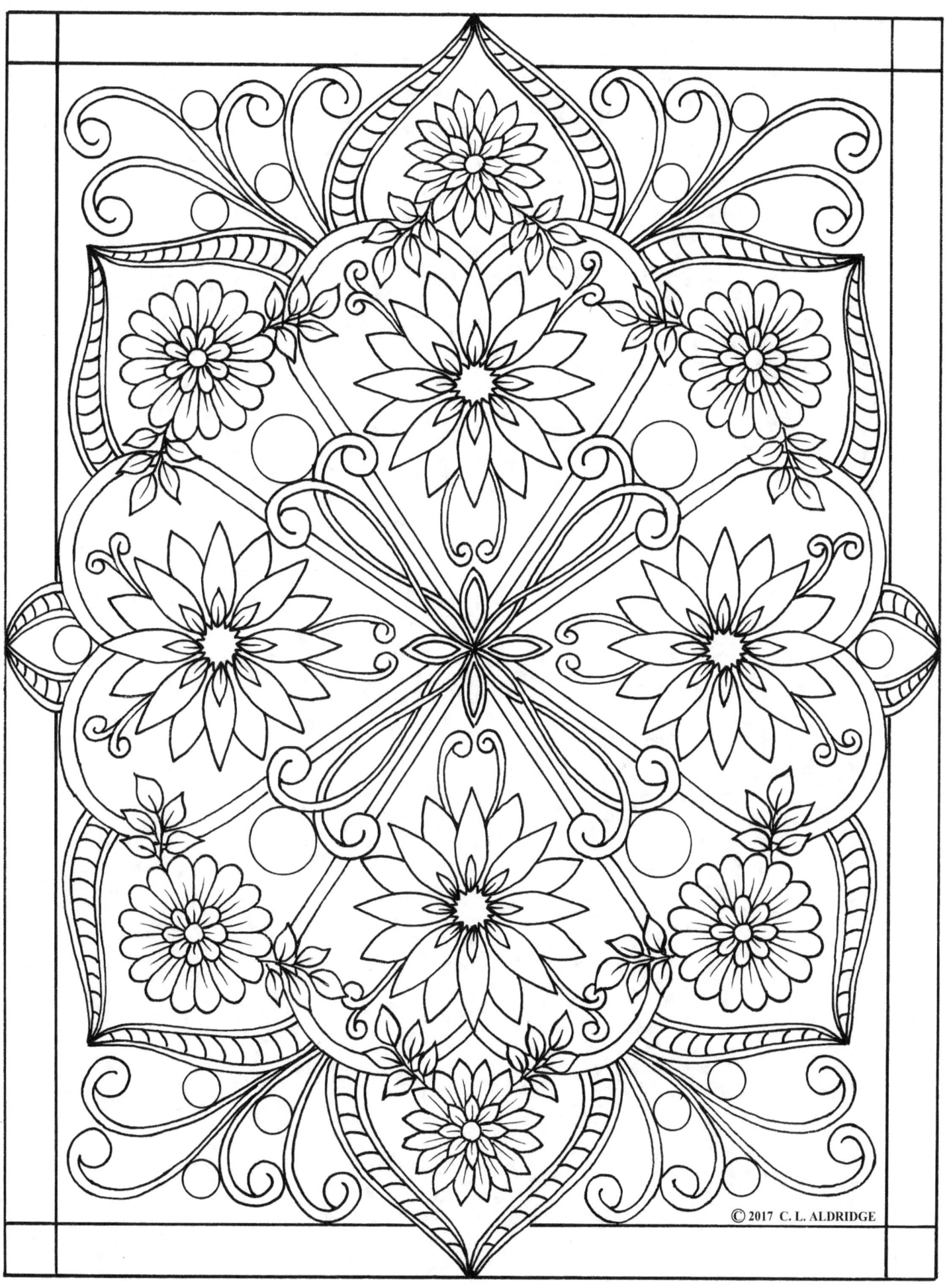

© 2017 C. L. ALDRIDGE

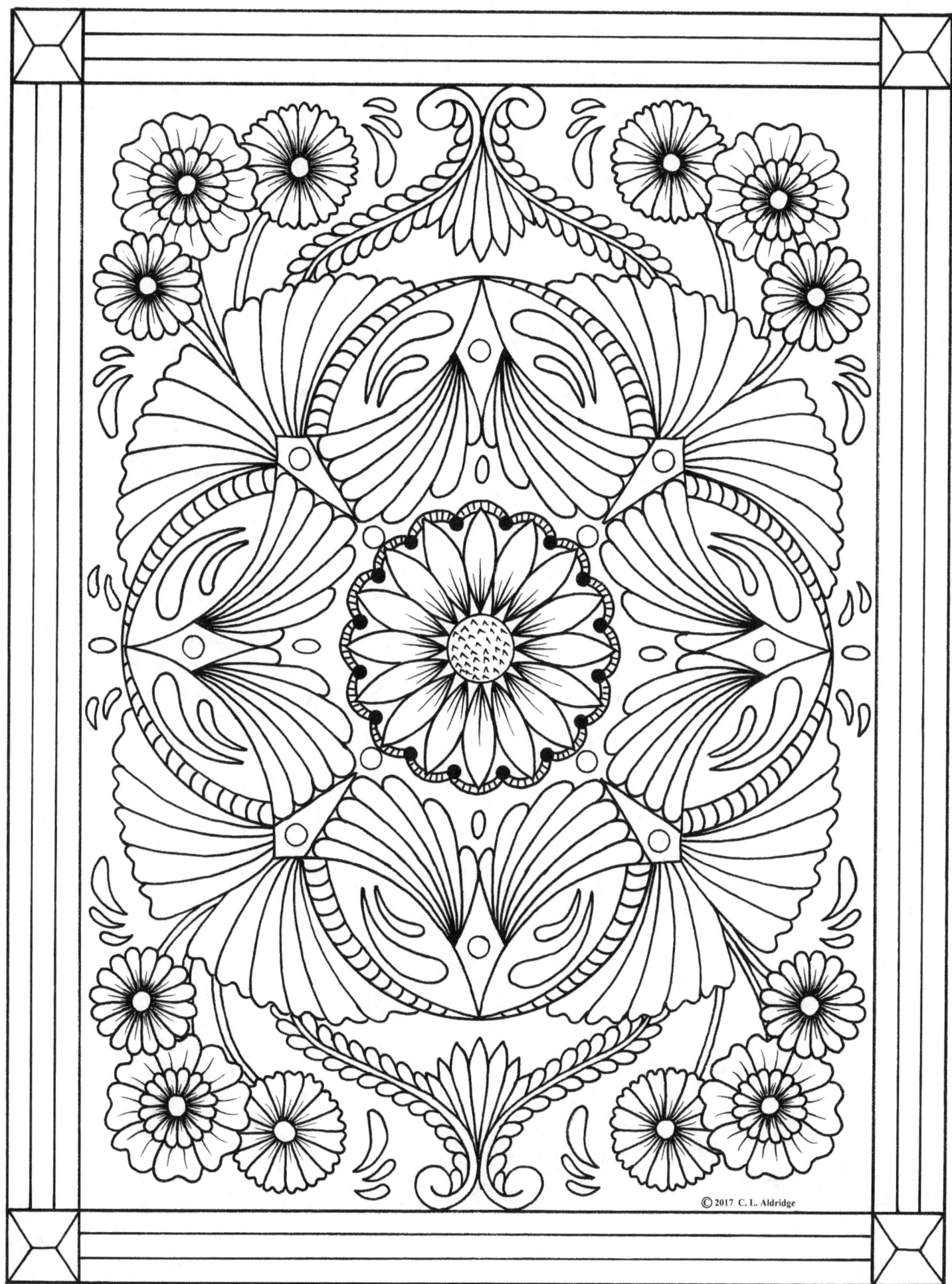

© 2017 C. L. Aldridge

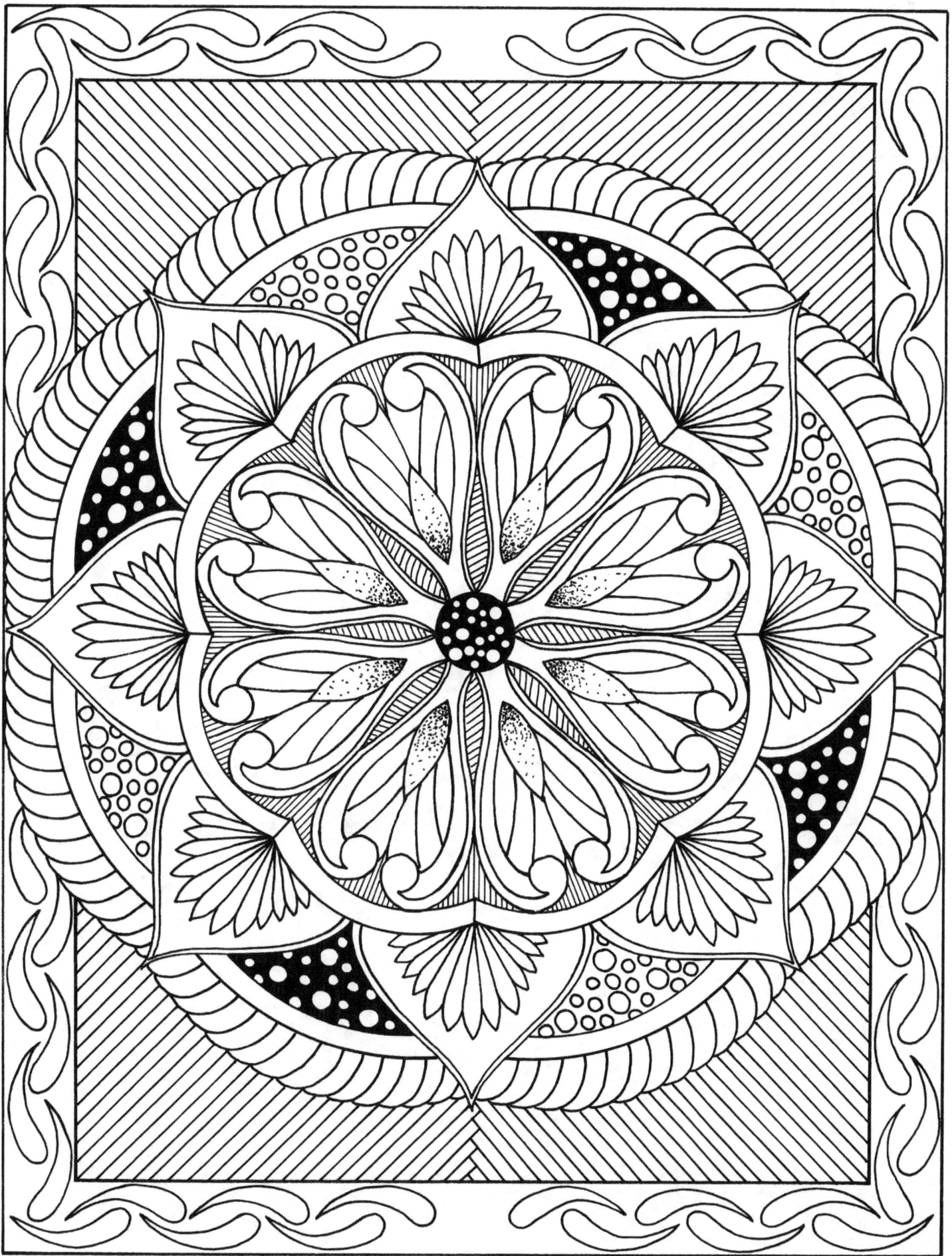

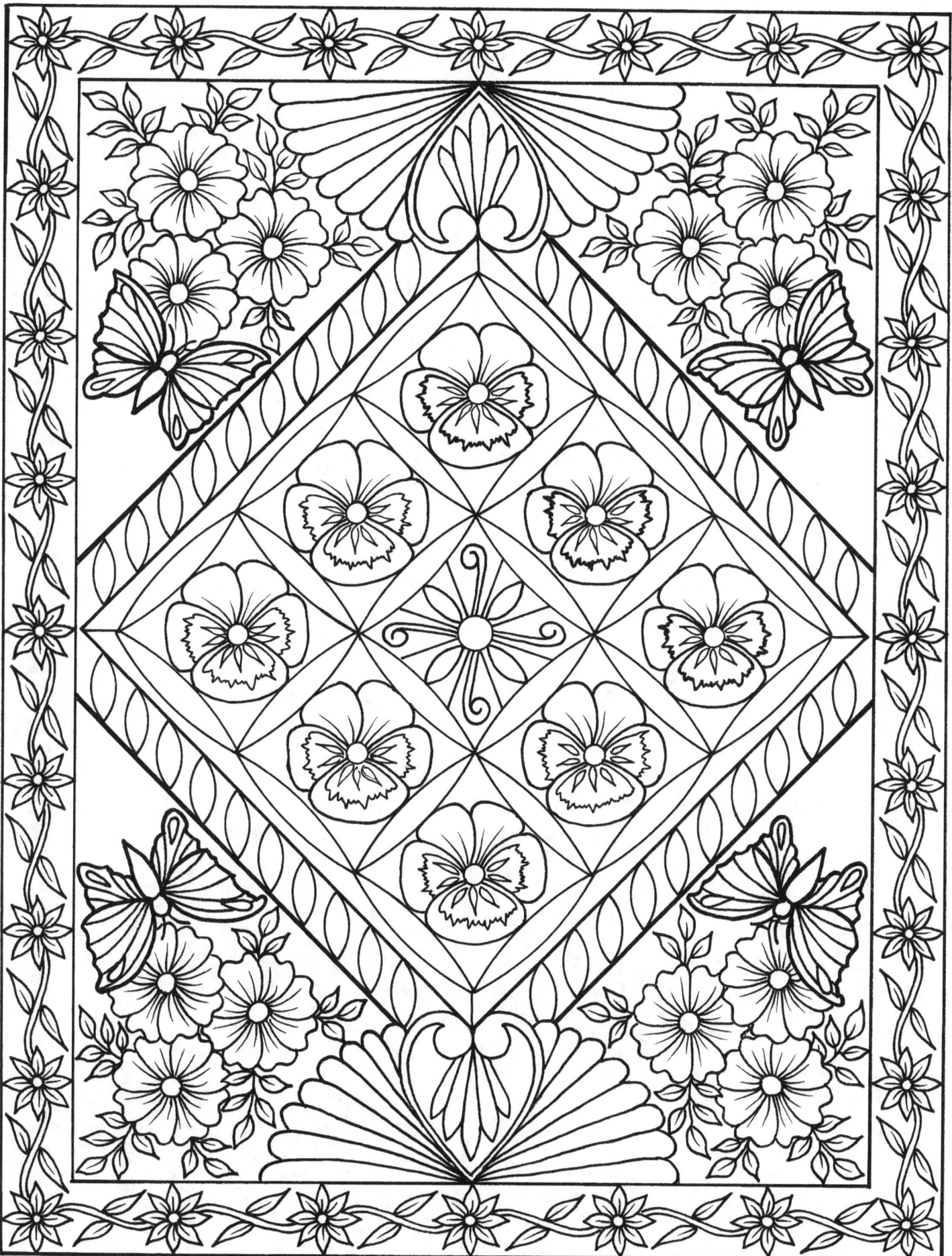

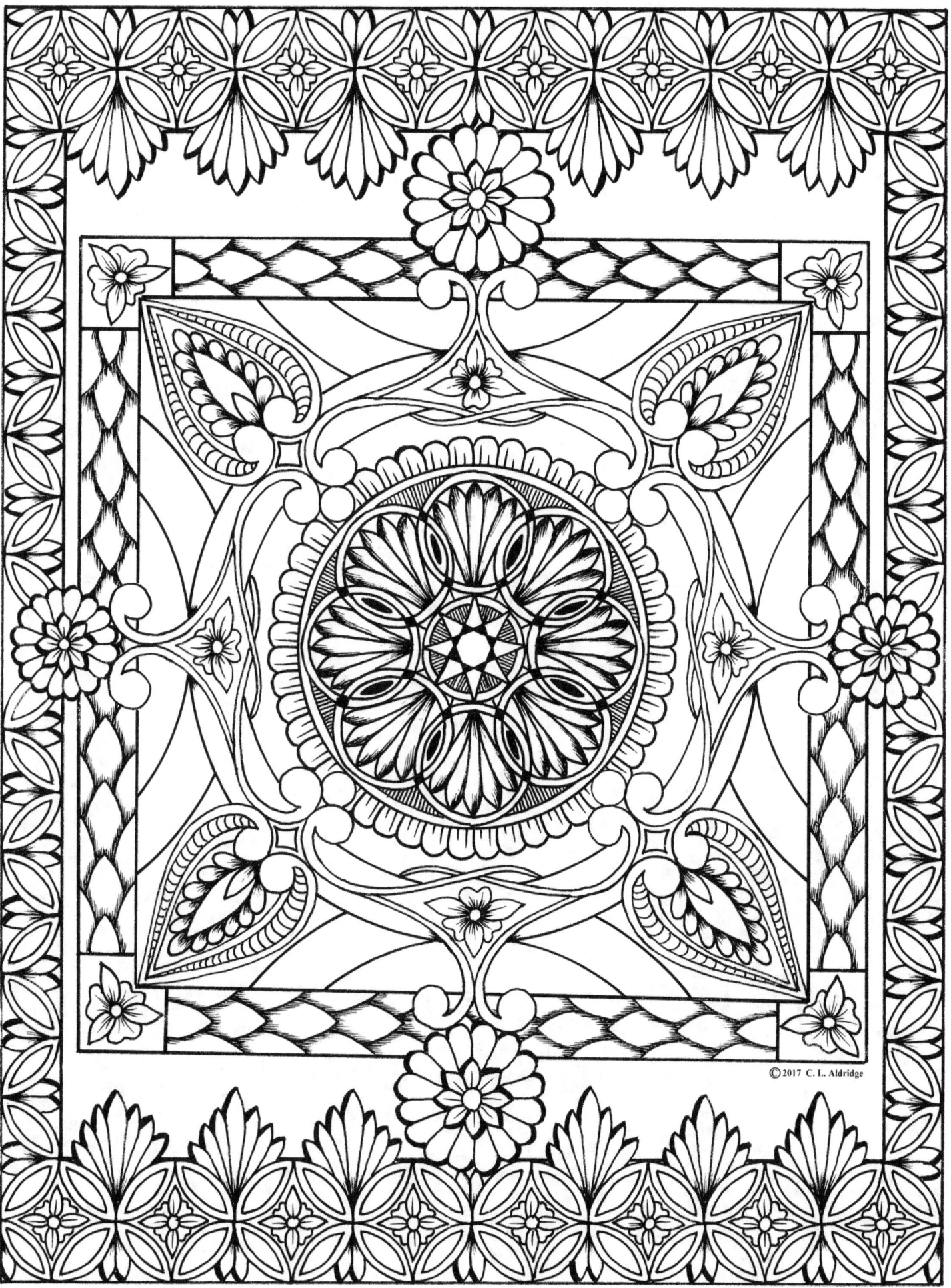

©2017 C. L. Aldridge

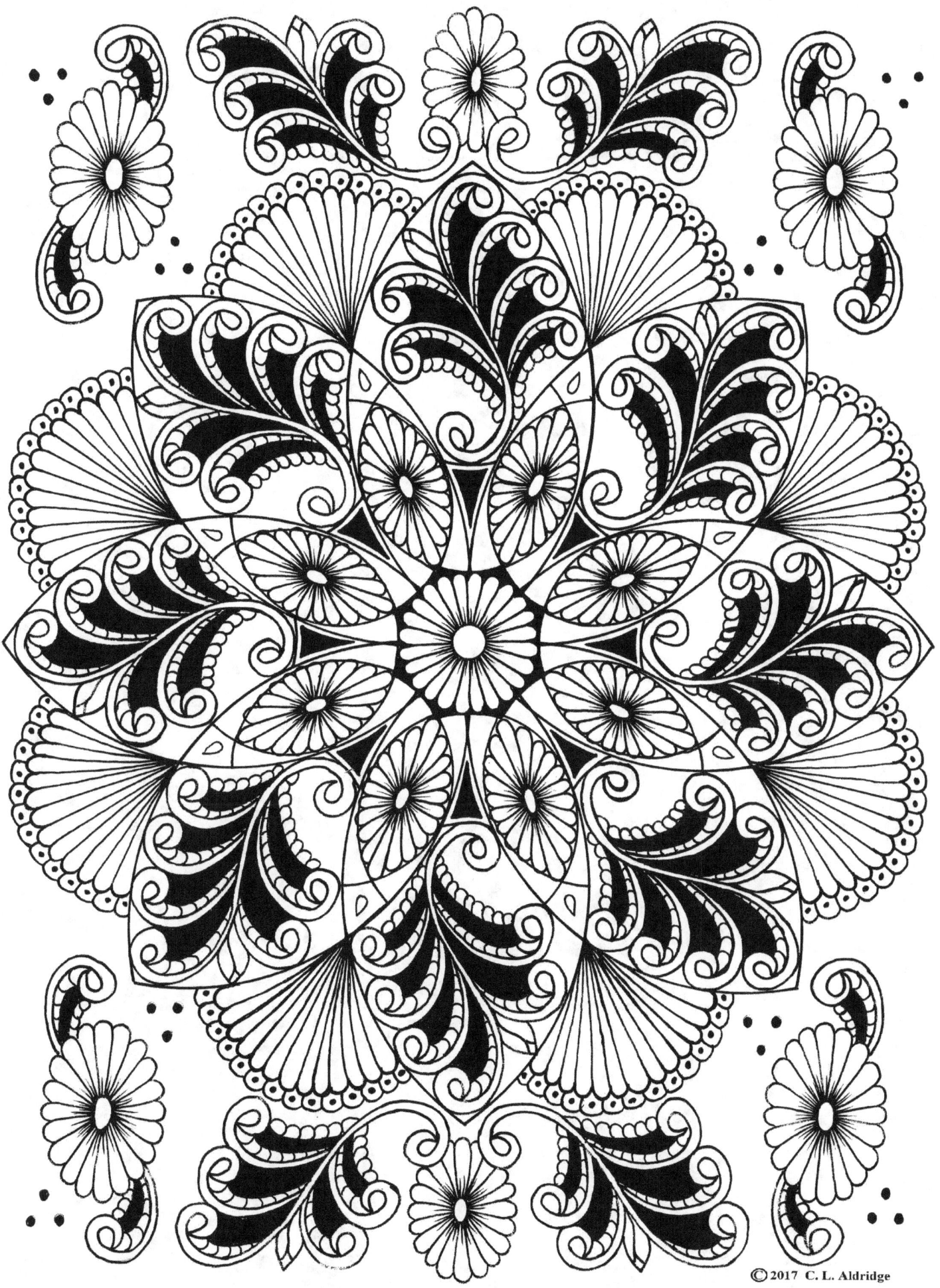

© 2017 C. L. Aldridge

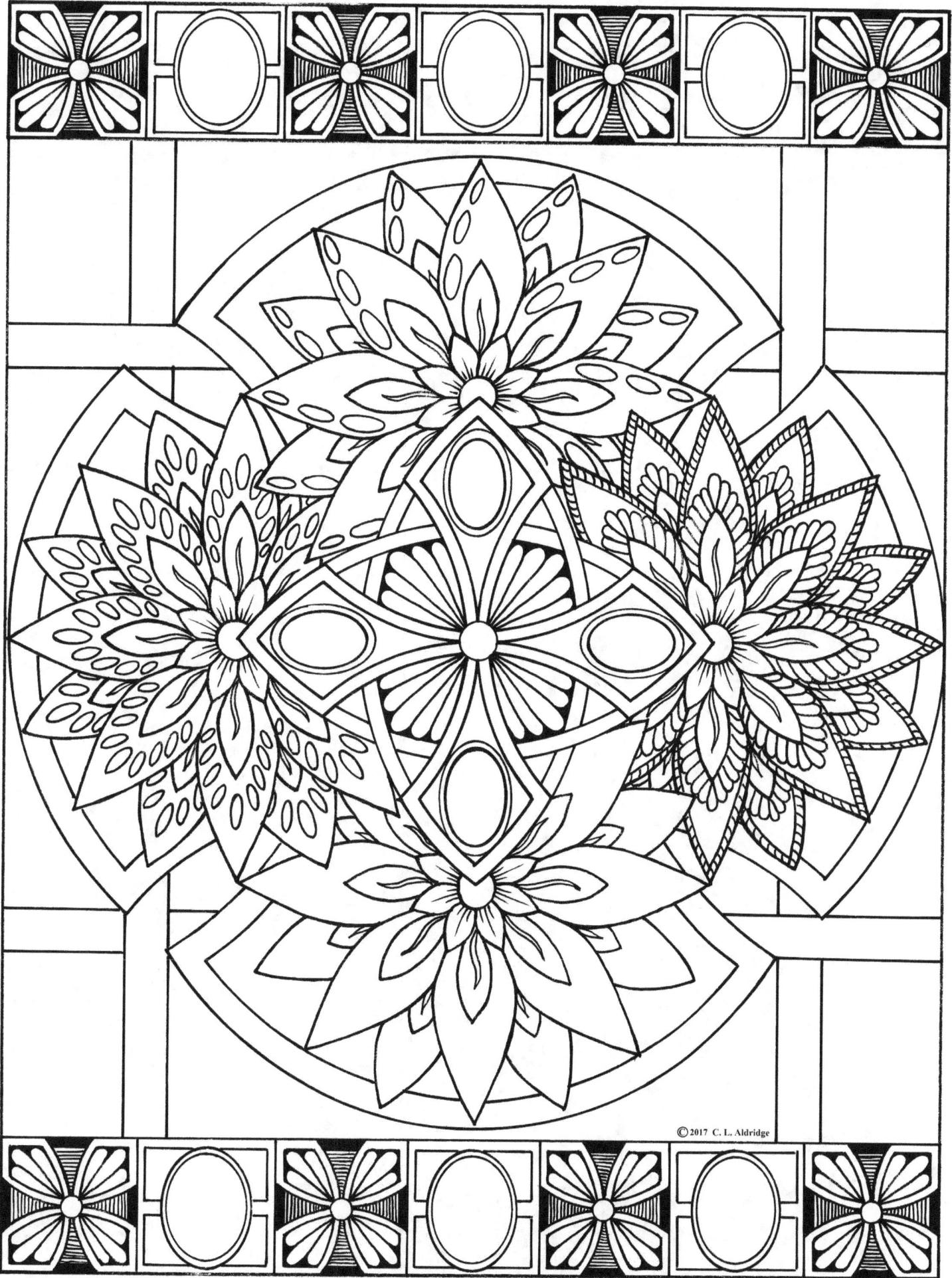

© 2017 C. L. Aldridge

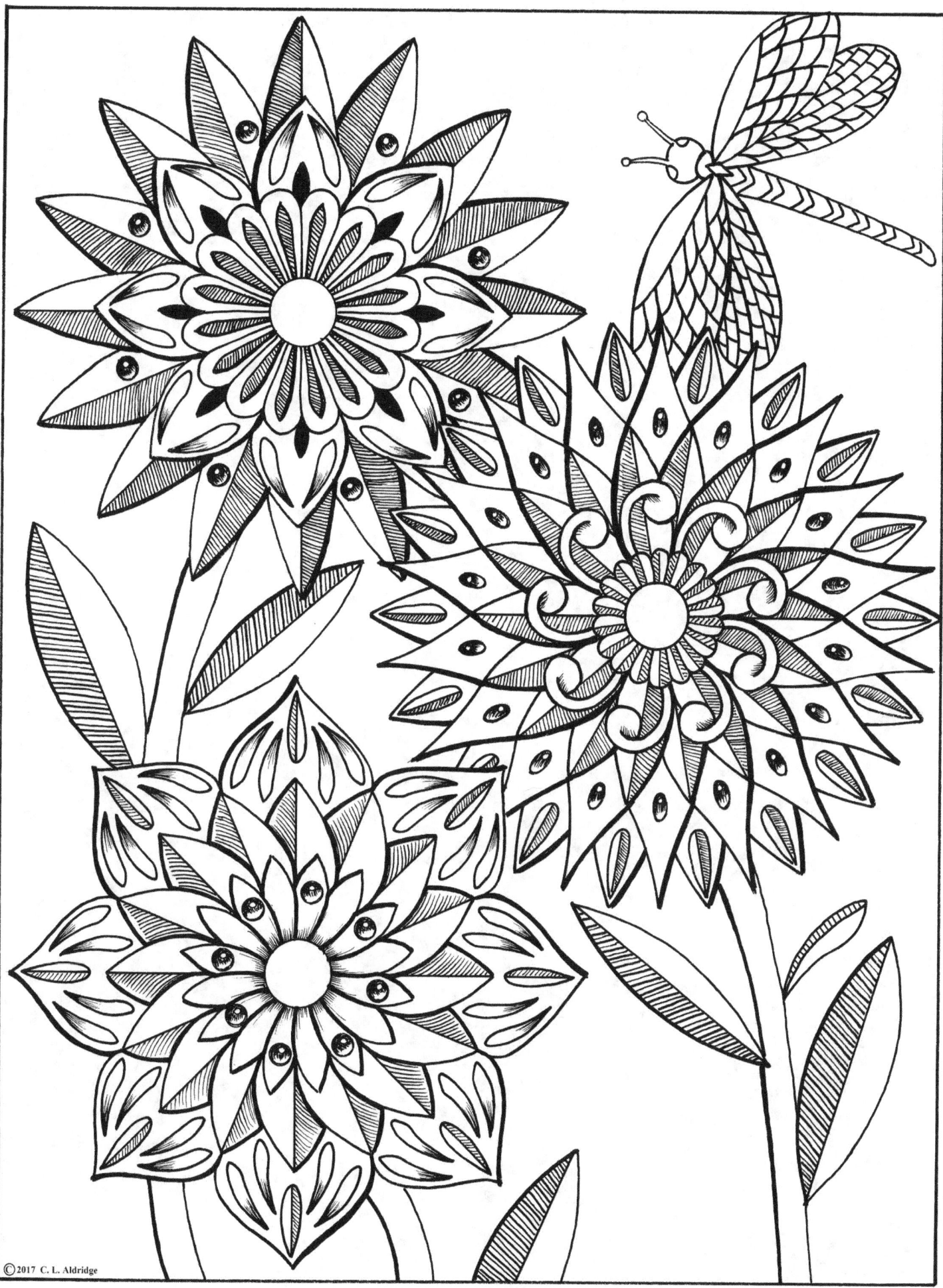

© 2017 C. L. Aldridge

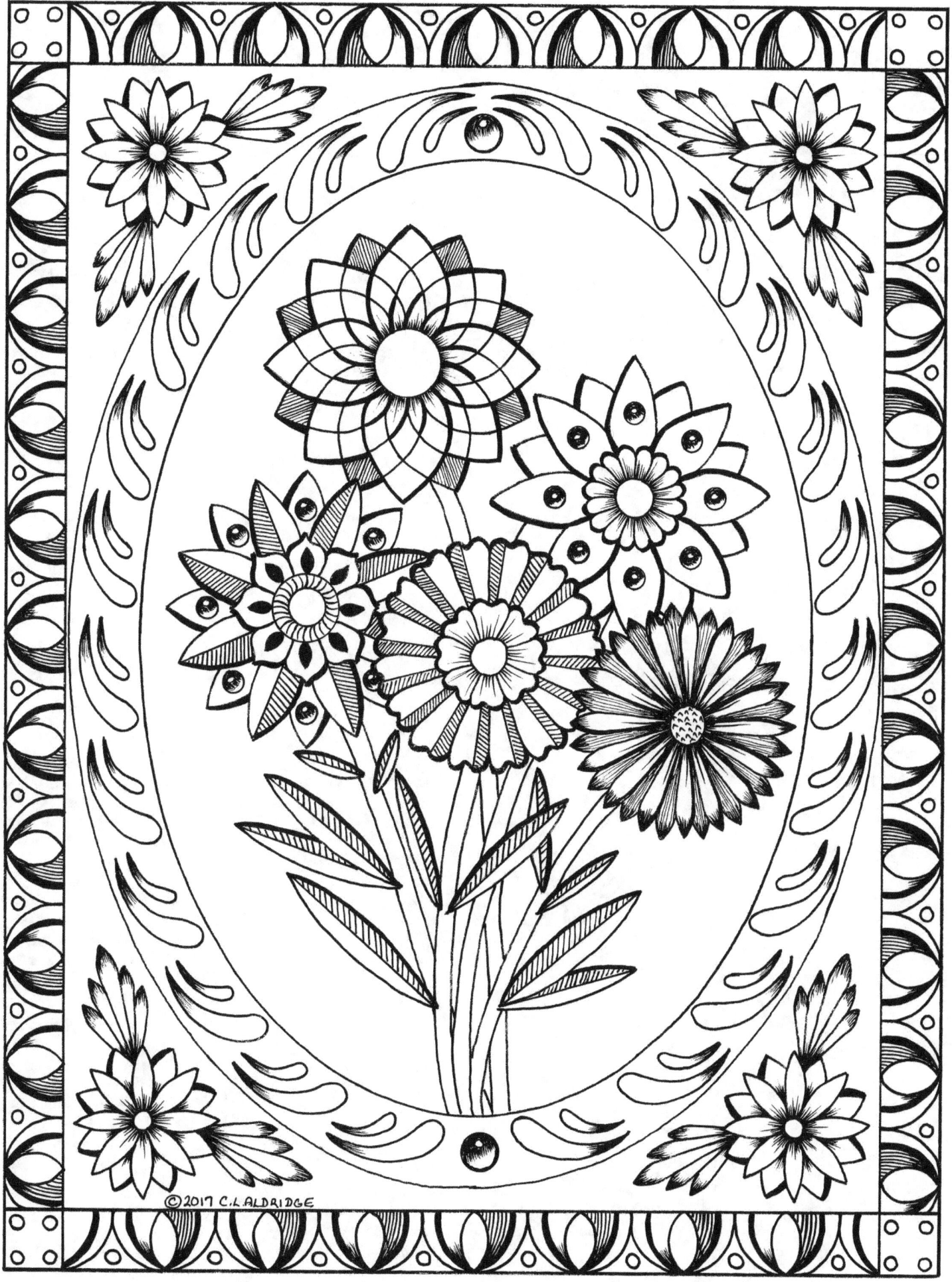

©2017 C.L.ALDRIDGE

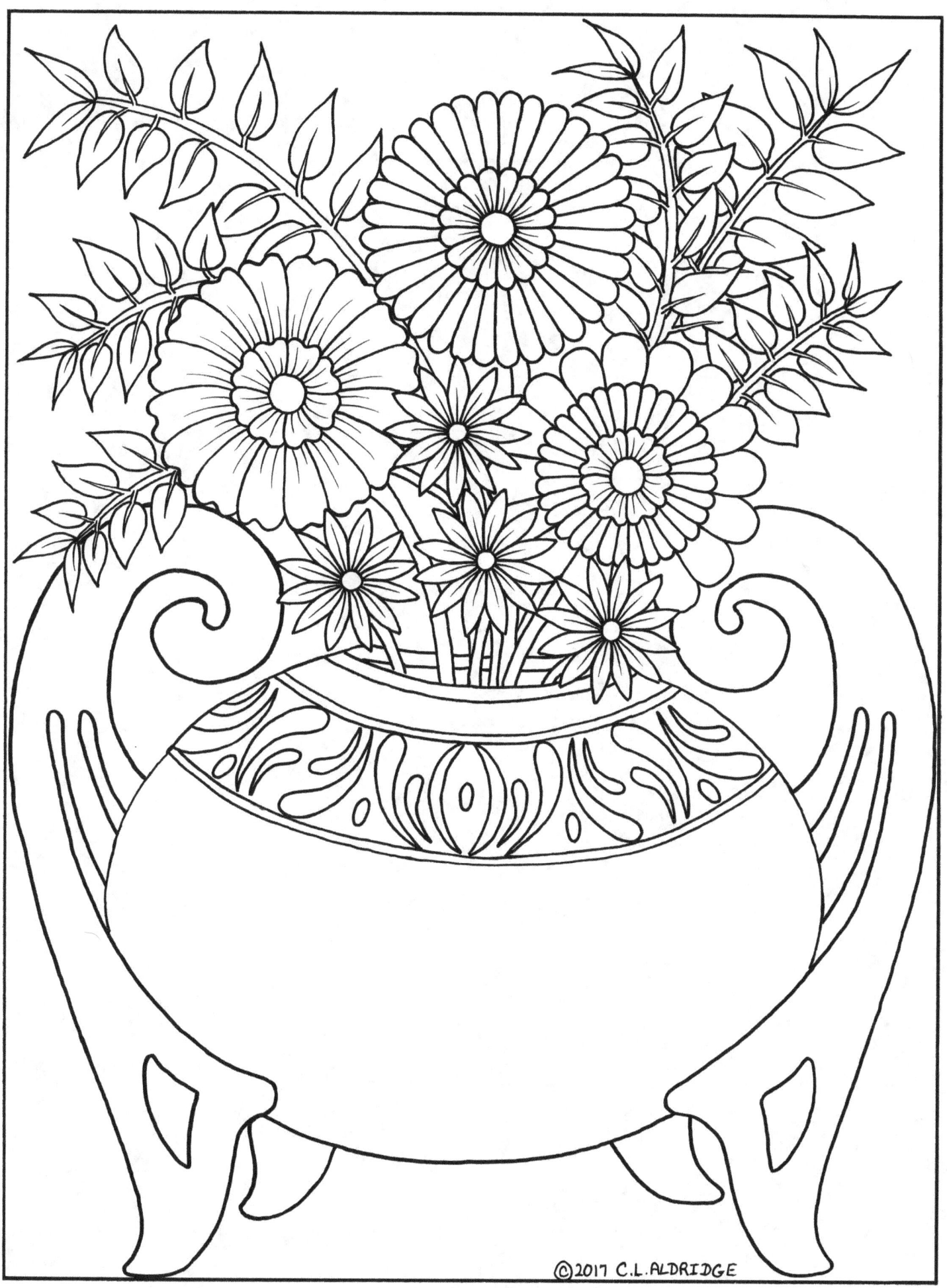

©2017 C.L.ALDRIDGE

© 2017 C. L. ALDRIDGE

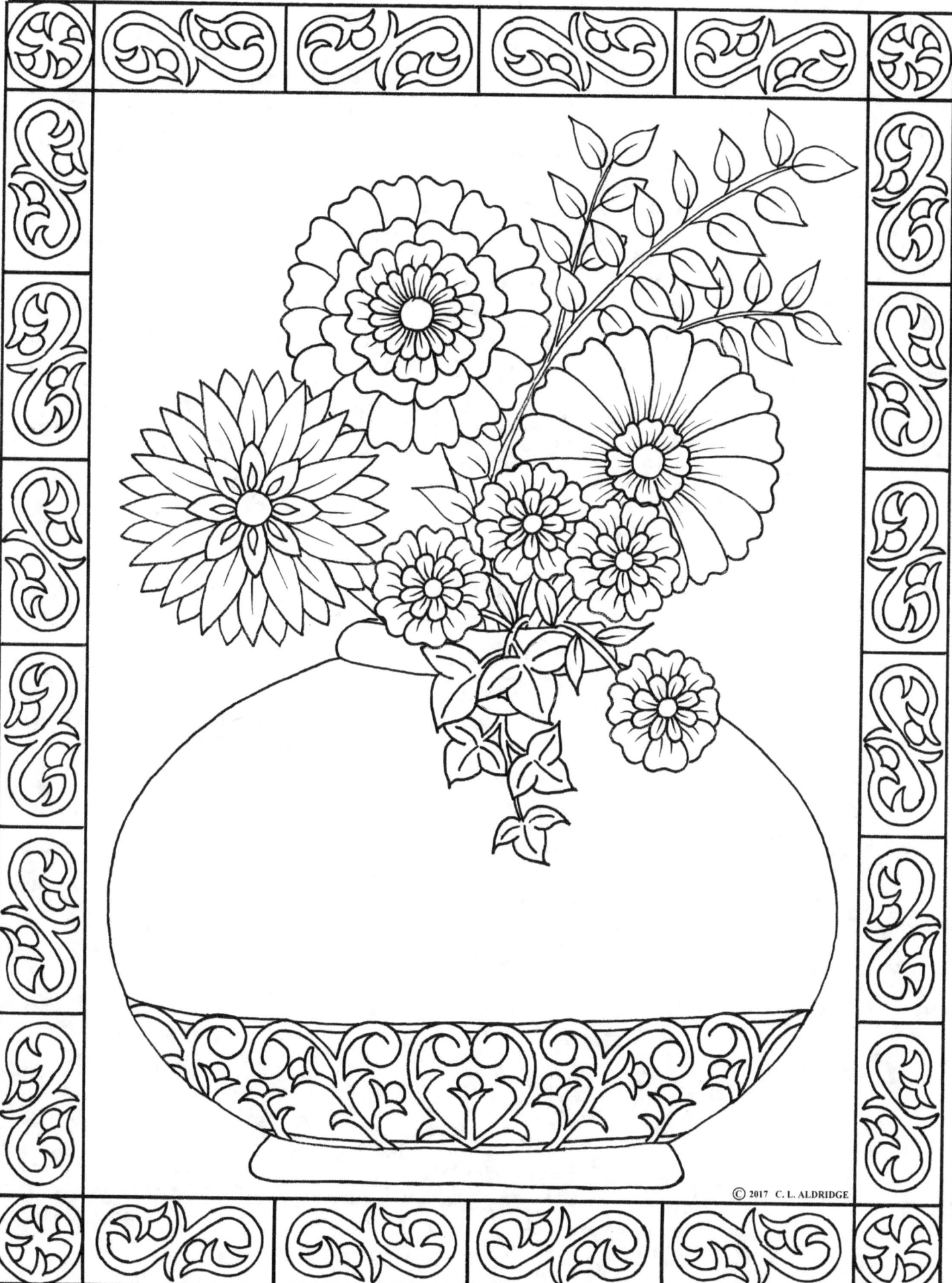

© 2017 C. L. ALDRIDGE

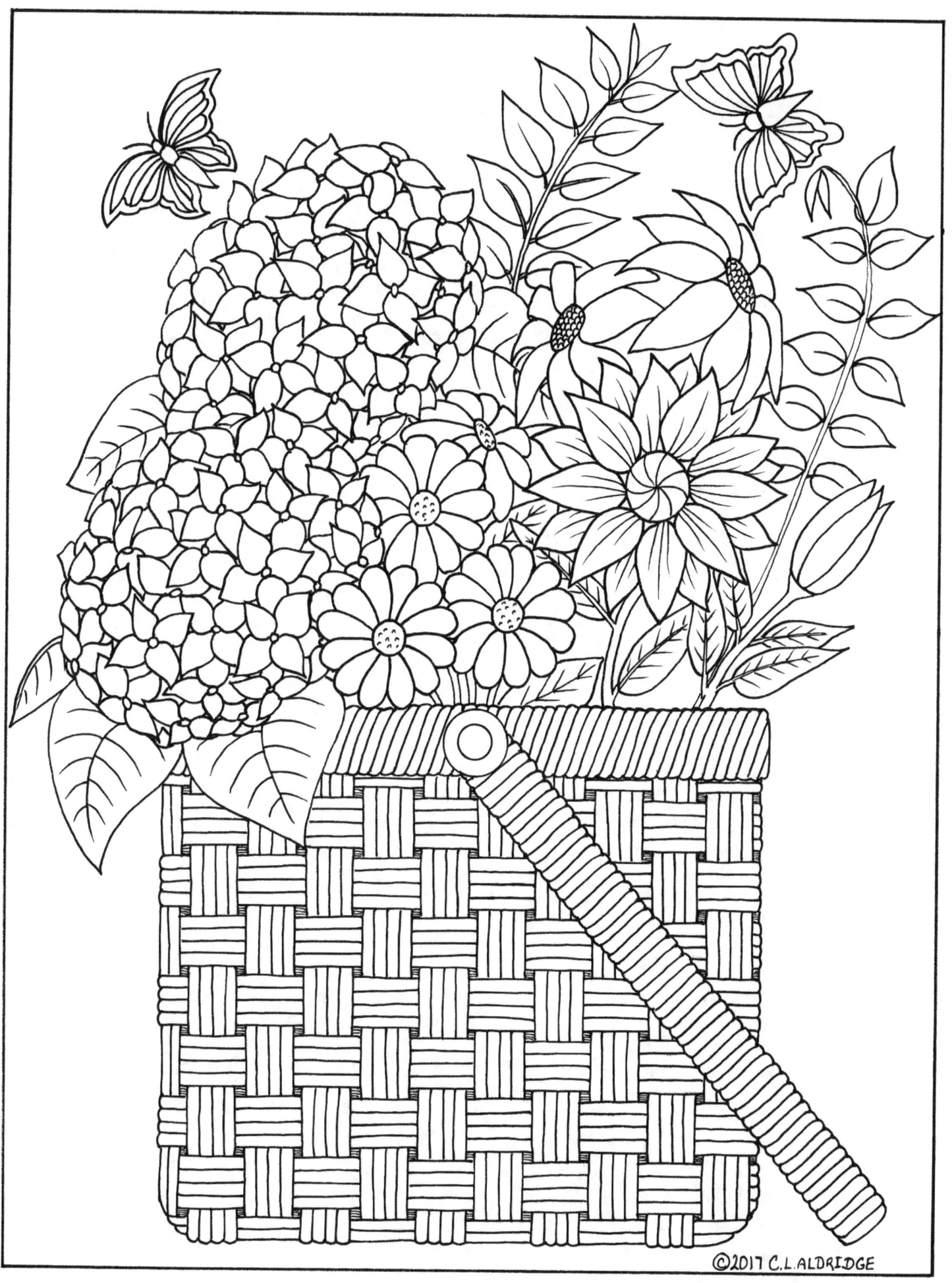

©2017 C.L.ALDRIDGE

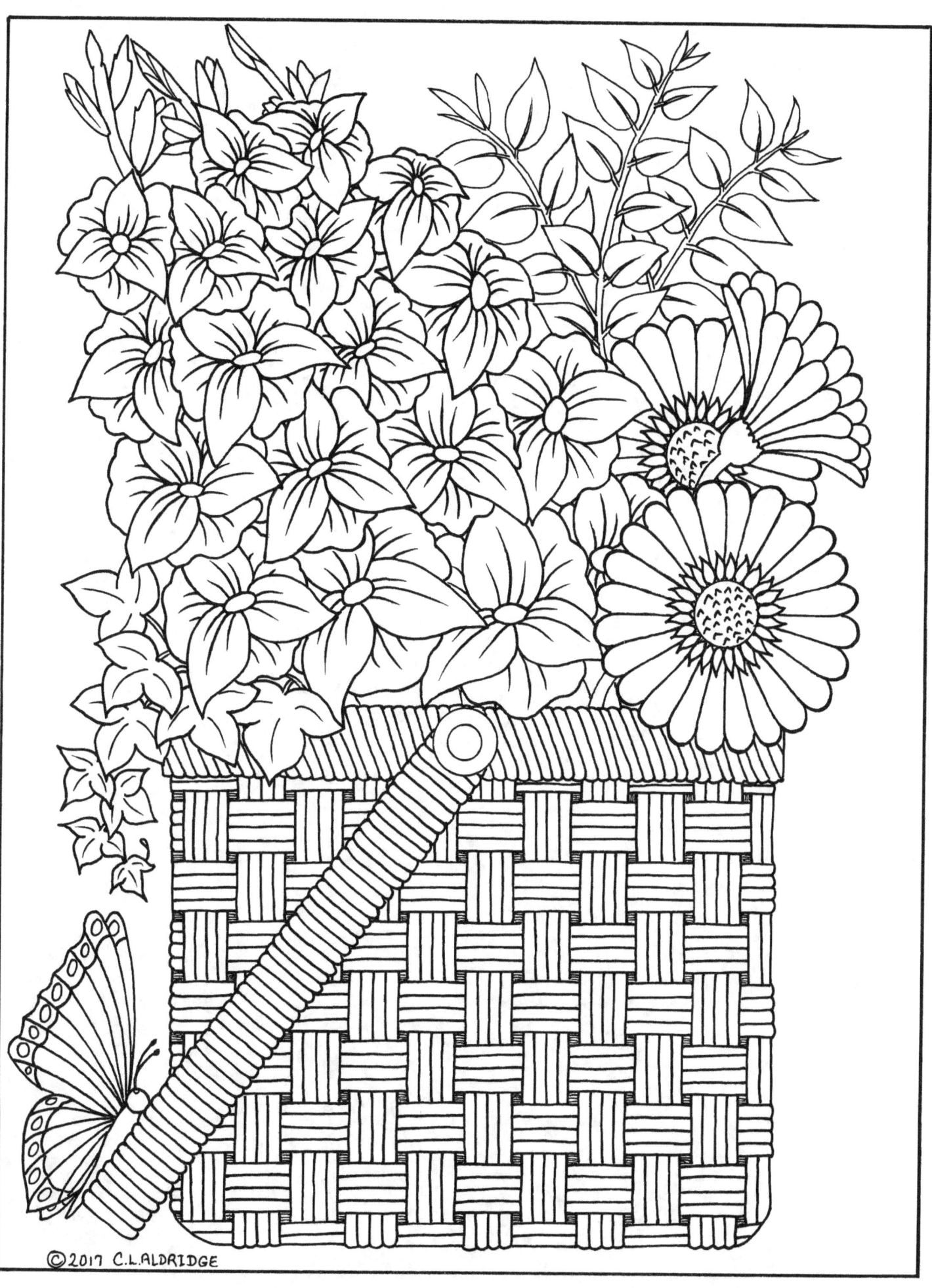

©2017 C.L.ALDRIDGE

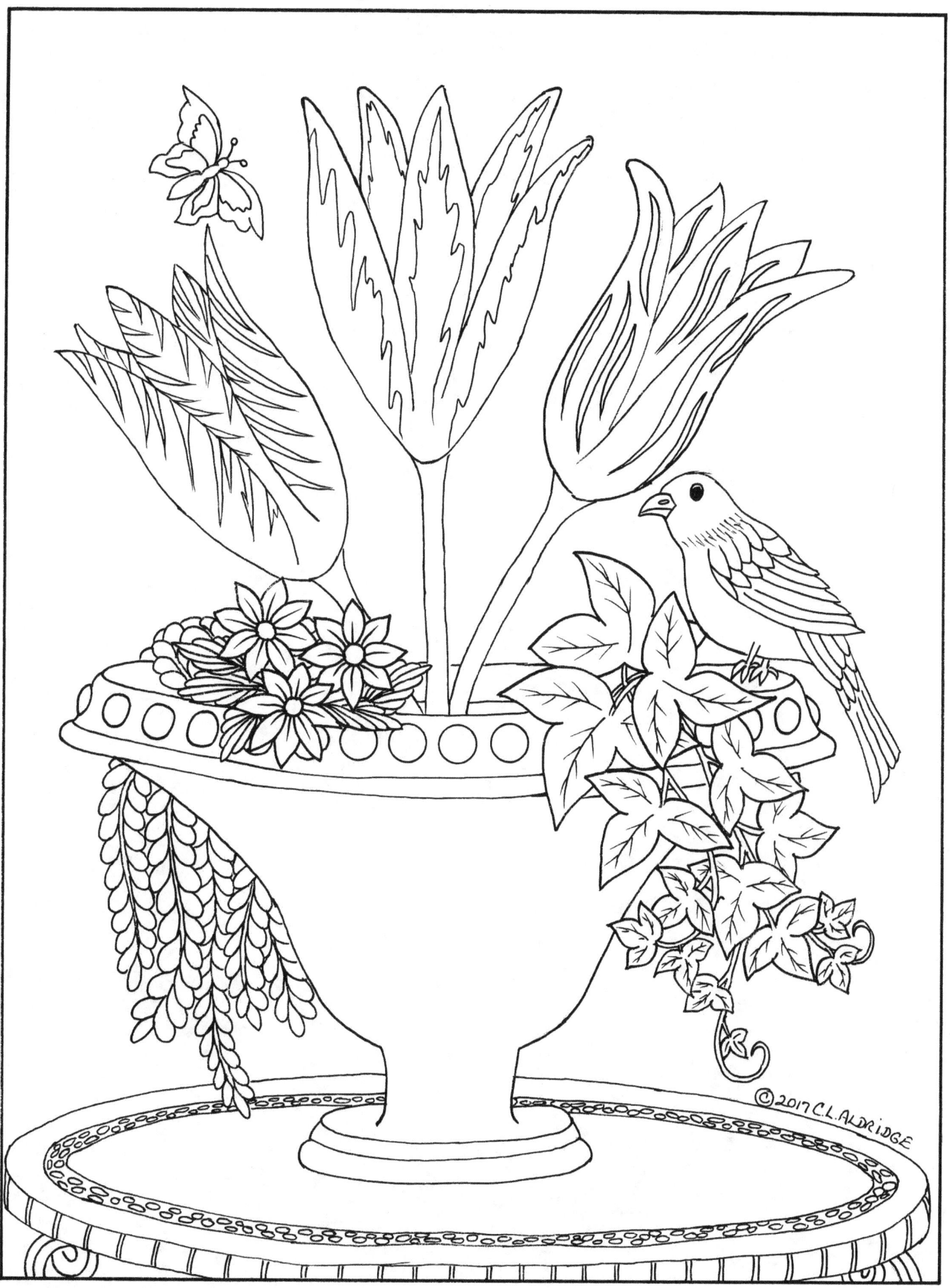

©2017 C.L.ALDRIDGE

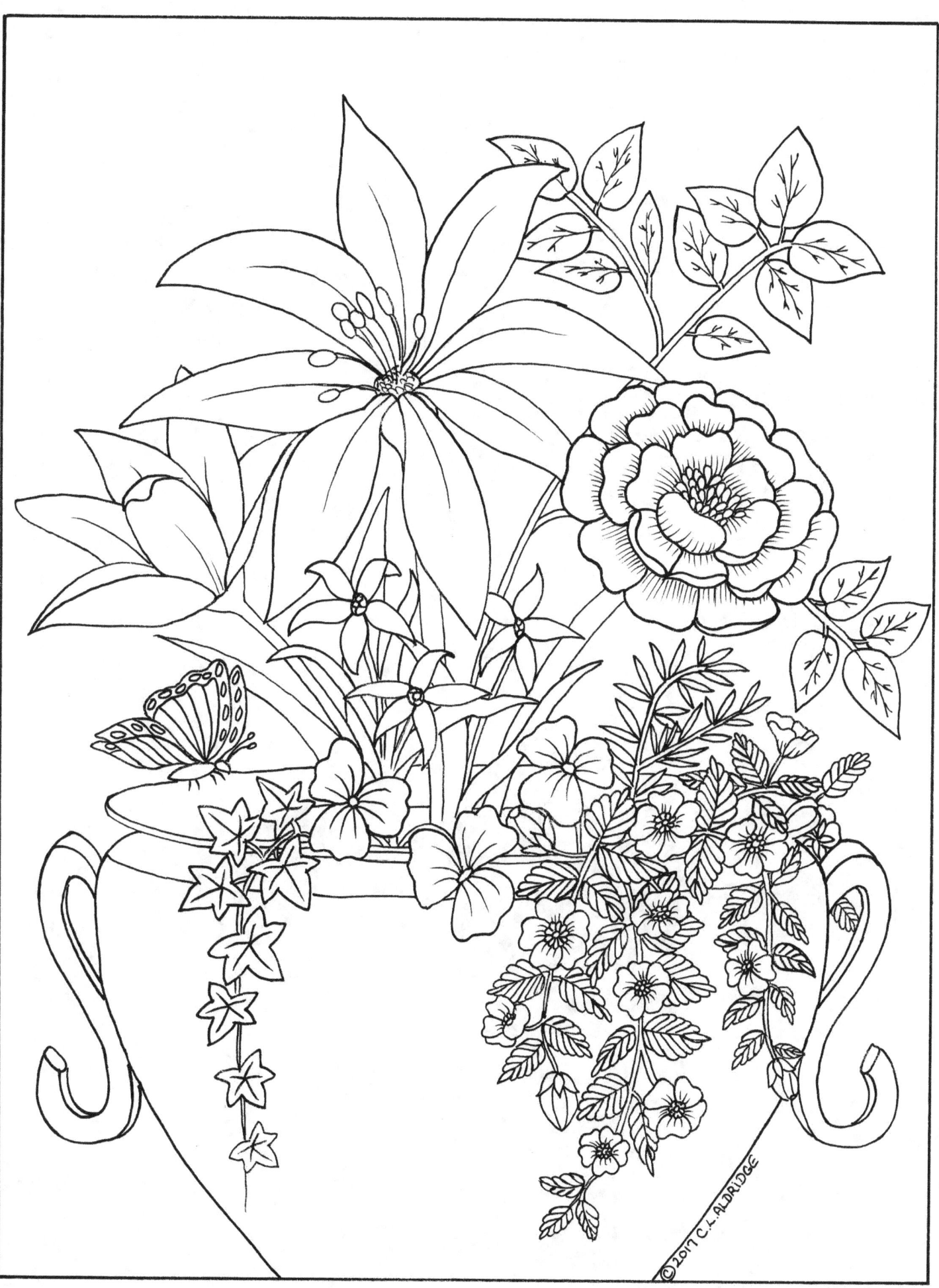
©2017 C.L. ALDRIDGE

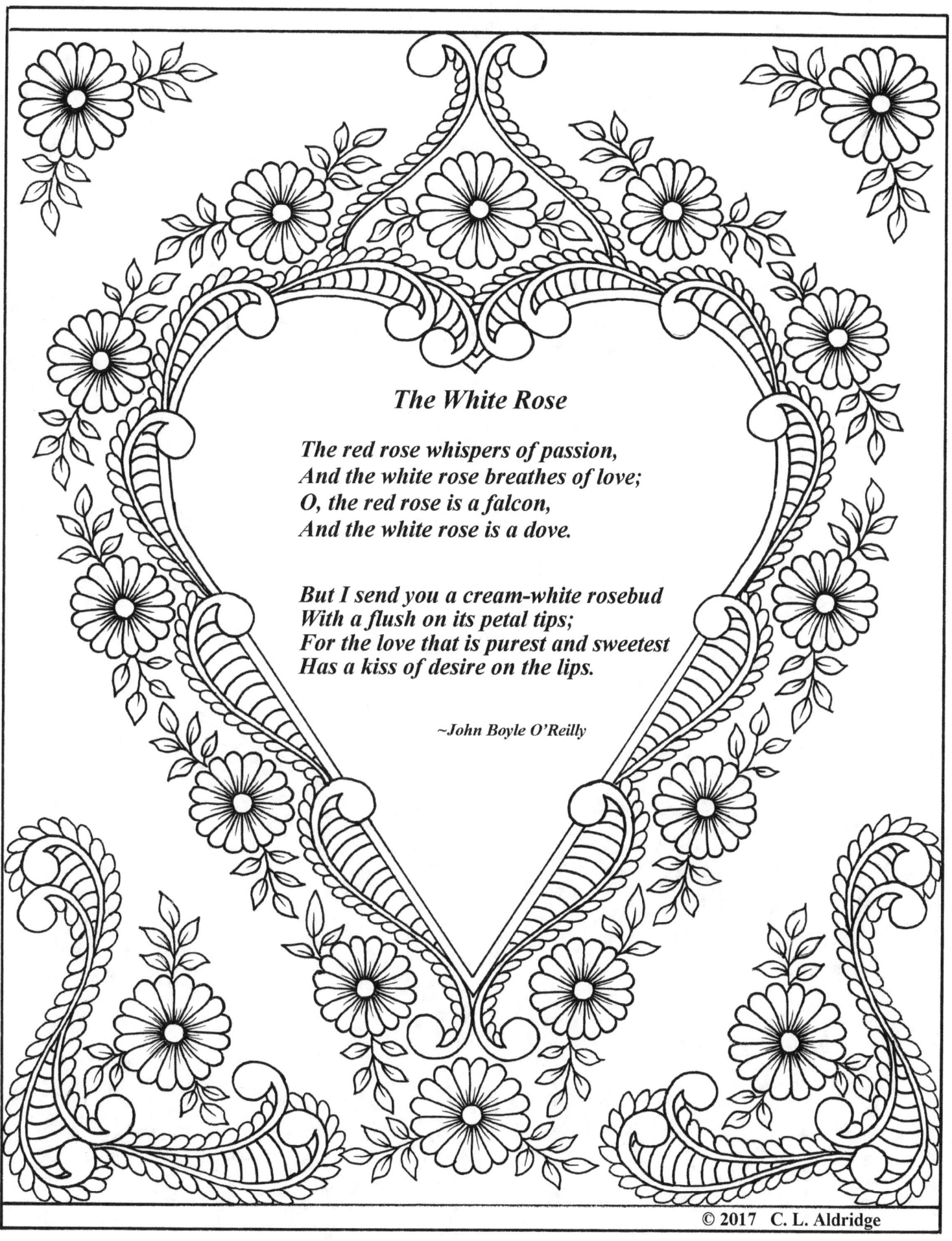

The White Rose

The red rose whispers of passion,
And the white rose breathes of love;
O, the red rose is a falcon,
And the white rose is a dove.

But I send you a cream-white rosebud
With a flush on its petal tips;
For the love that is purest and sweetest
Has a kiss of desire on the lips.

~John Boyle O'Reilly

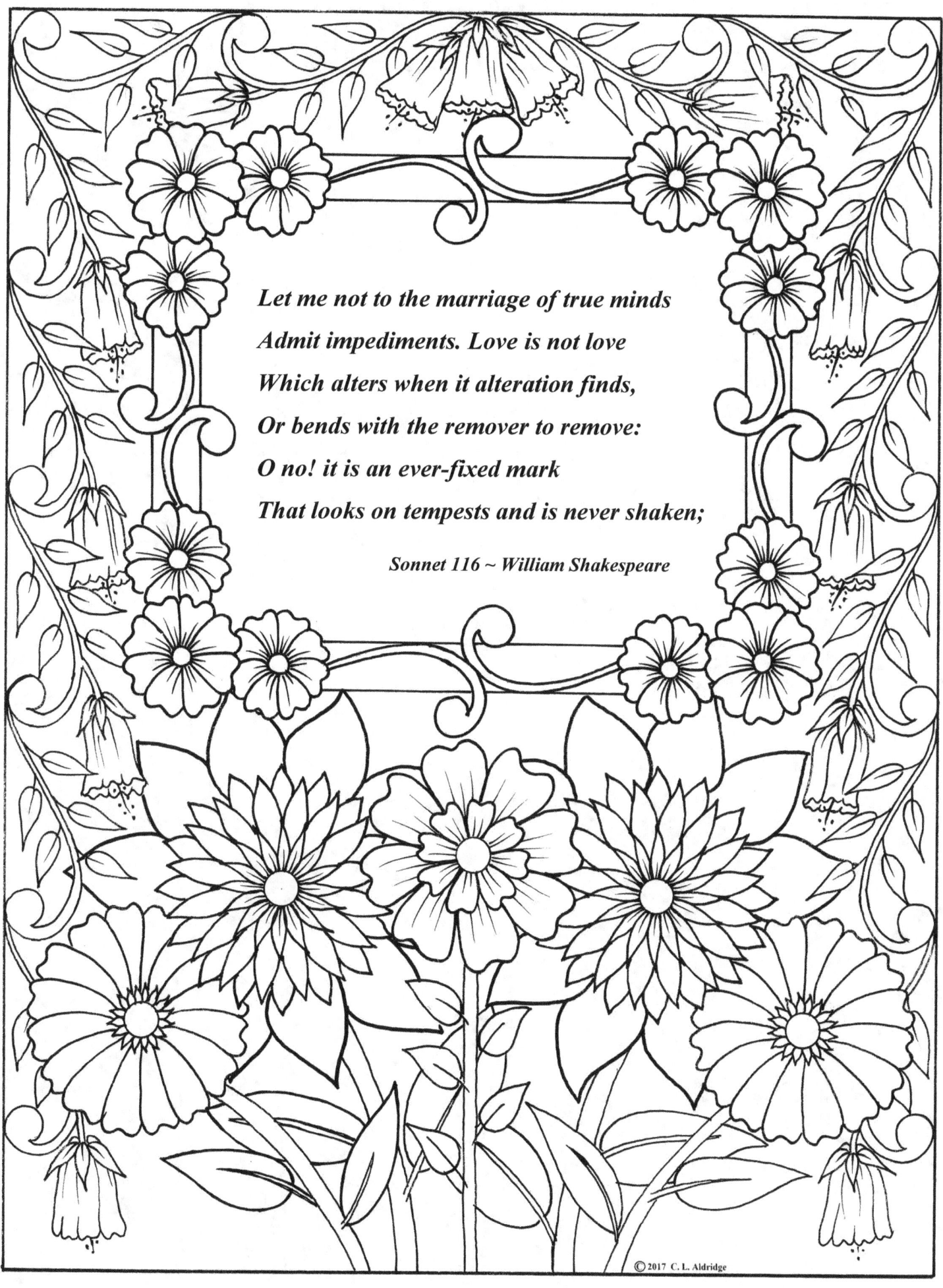

Let me not to the marriage of true minds

Admit impediments. Love is not love

Which alters when it alteration finds,

Or bends with the remover to remove:

O no! it is an ever-fixed mark

That looks on tempests and is never shaken;

Sonnet 116 ~ William Shakespeare

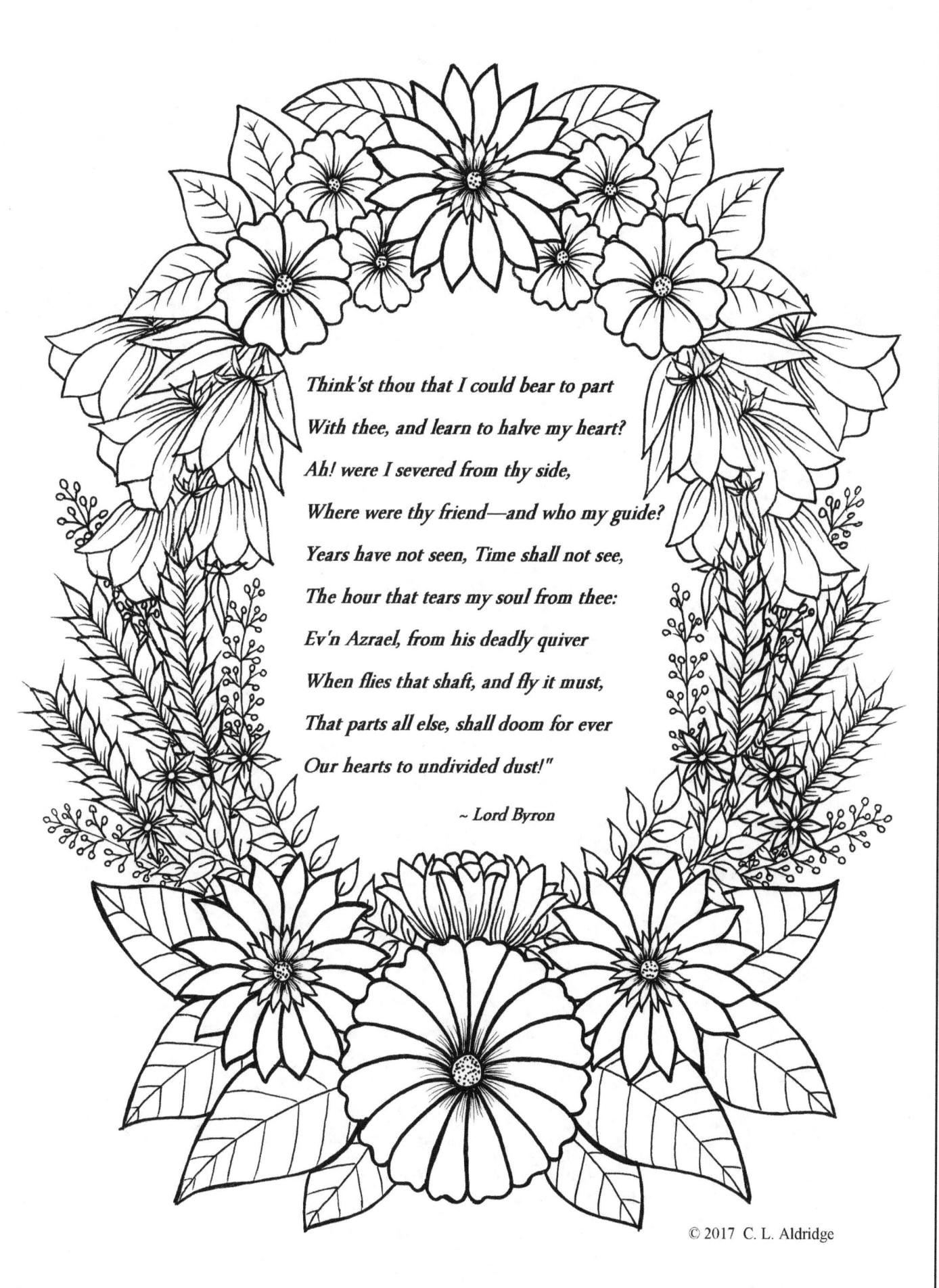

Think'st thou that I could bear to part

With thee, and learn to halve my heart?

Ah! were I severed from thy side,

Where were thy friend—and who my guide?

Years have not seen, Time shall not see,

The hour that tears my soul from thee:

Ev'n Azrael, from his deadly quiver

When flies that shaft, and fly it must,

That parts all else, shall doom for ever

Our hearts to undivided dust!"

~ Lord Byron

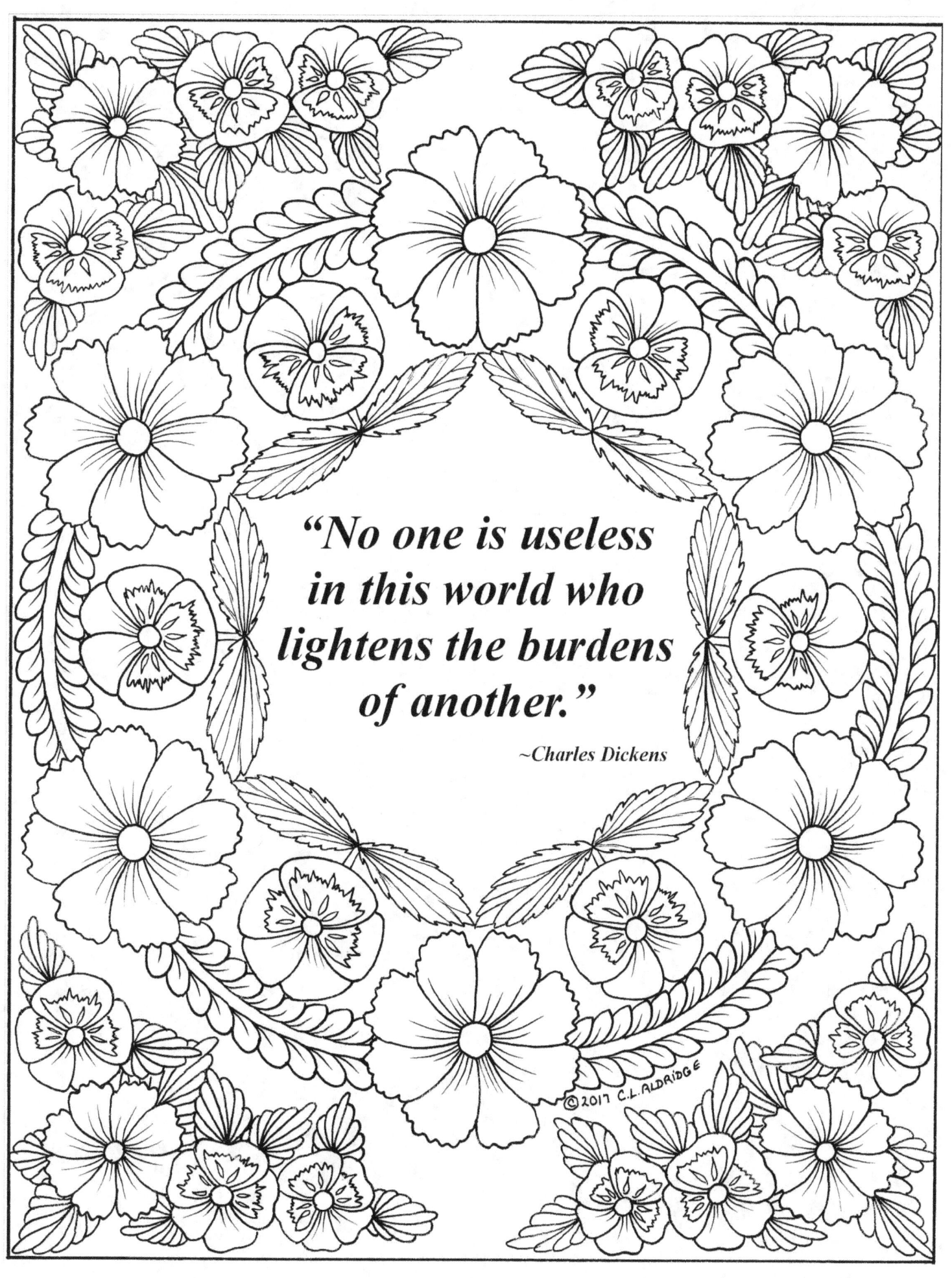

"No one is useless in this world who lightens the burdens of another."

~Charles Dickens

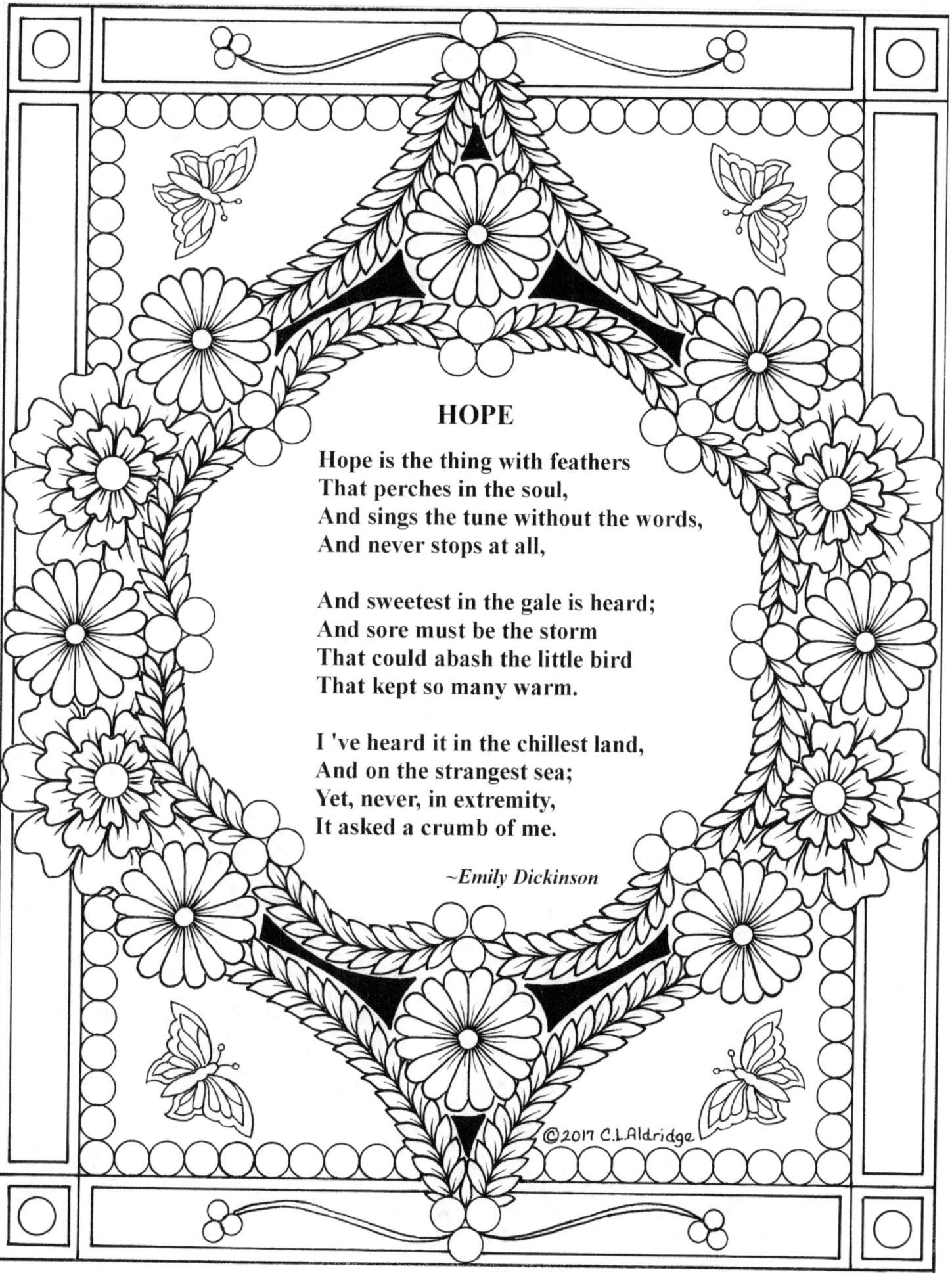

HOPE

Hope is the thing with feathers
That perches in the soul,
And sings the tune without the words,
And never stops at all,

And sweetest in the gale is heard;
And sore must be the storm
That could abash the little bird
That kept so many warm.

I 've heard it in the chillest land,
And on the strangest sea;
Yet, never, in extremity,
It asked a crumb of me.

~Emily Dickinson

©2017 C.L.Aldridge

A FULL SET OF
CRAFT/GREETING CARD
BONUS PAGES

Adapted versions of the larger drawings, perfect for framing (5" x 7"), or for crafting, scrapbooking, and making greeting cards!

Also great for working out your color schemes for the larger drawings.

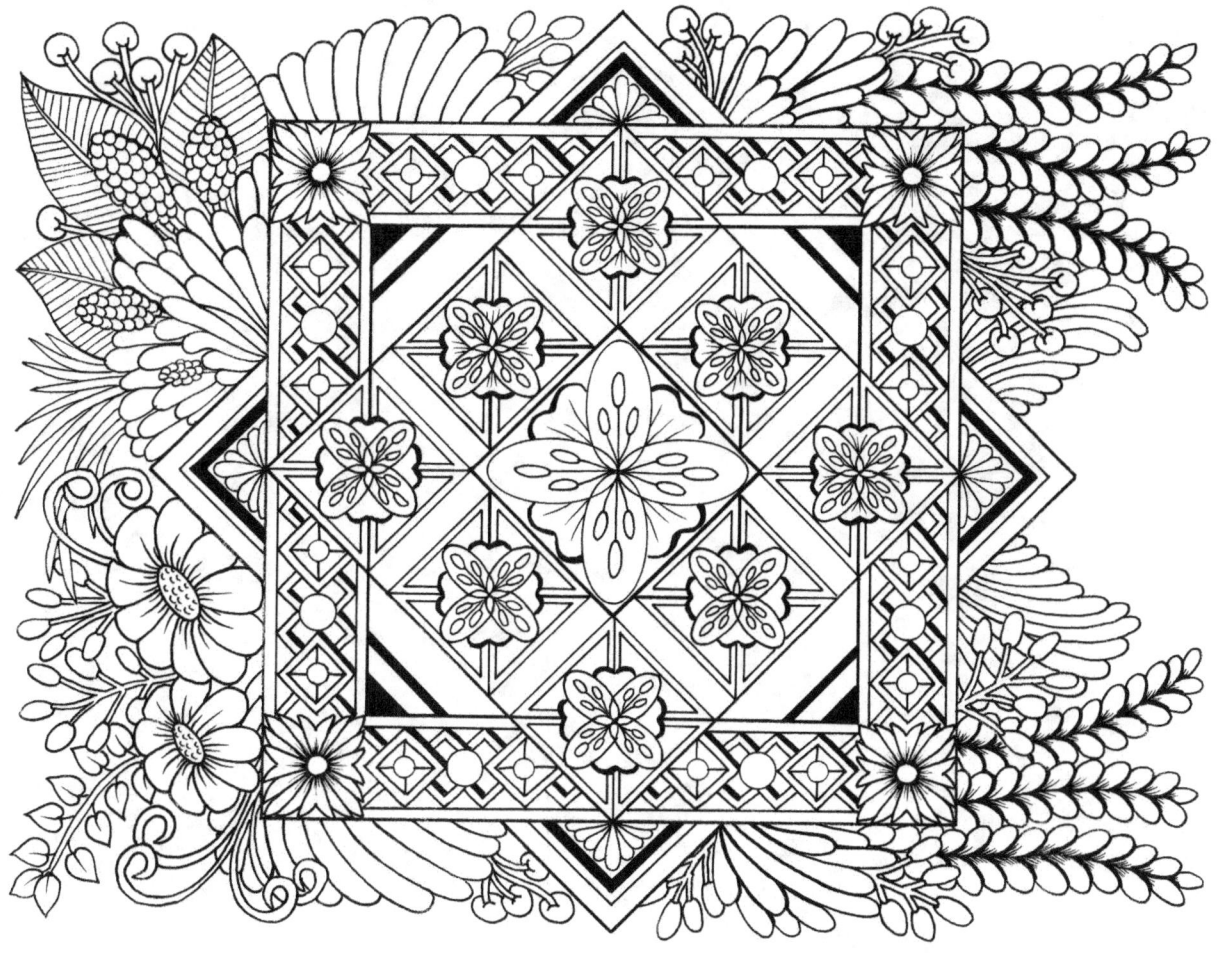

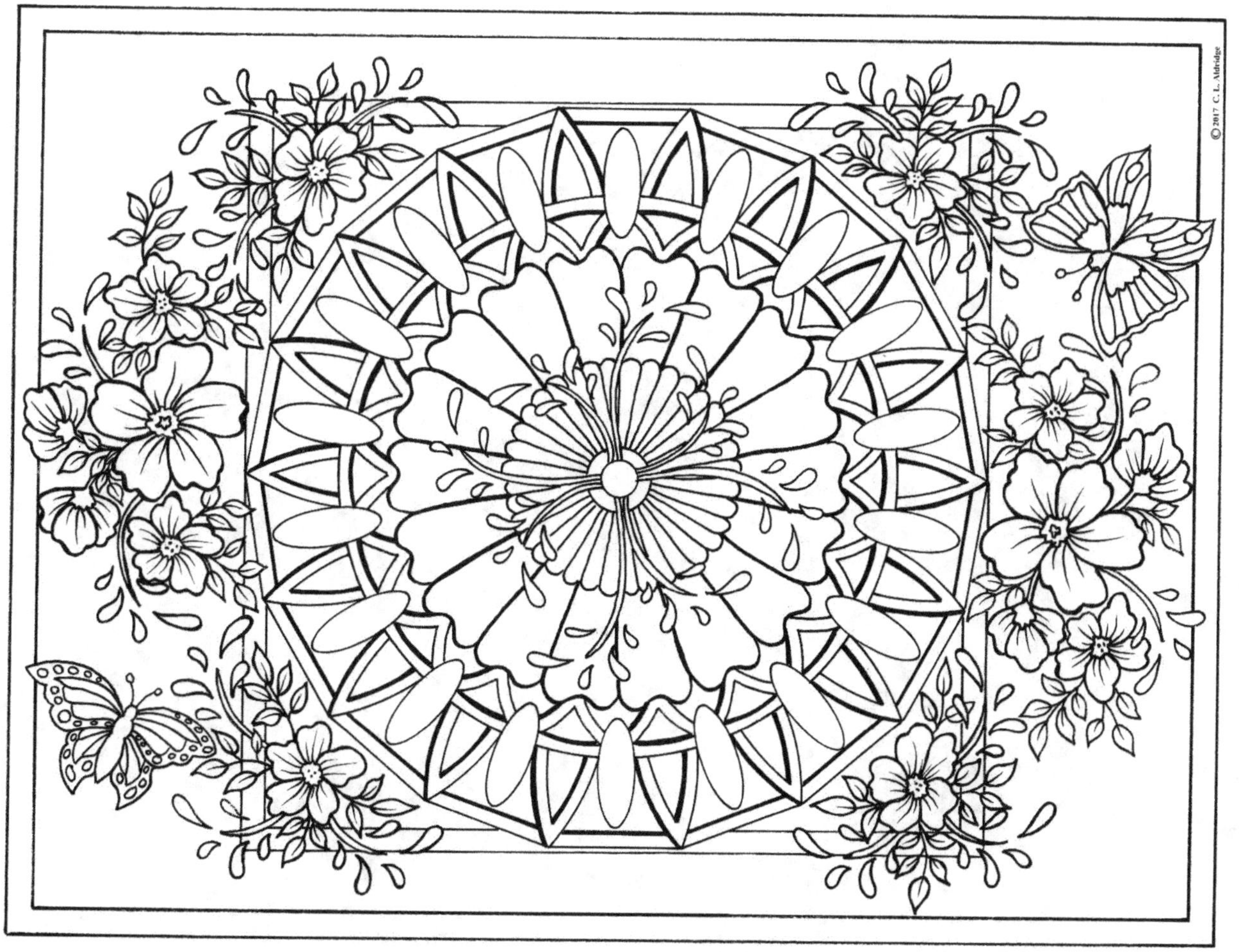

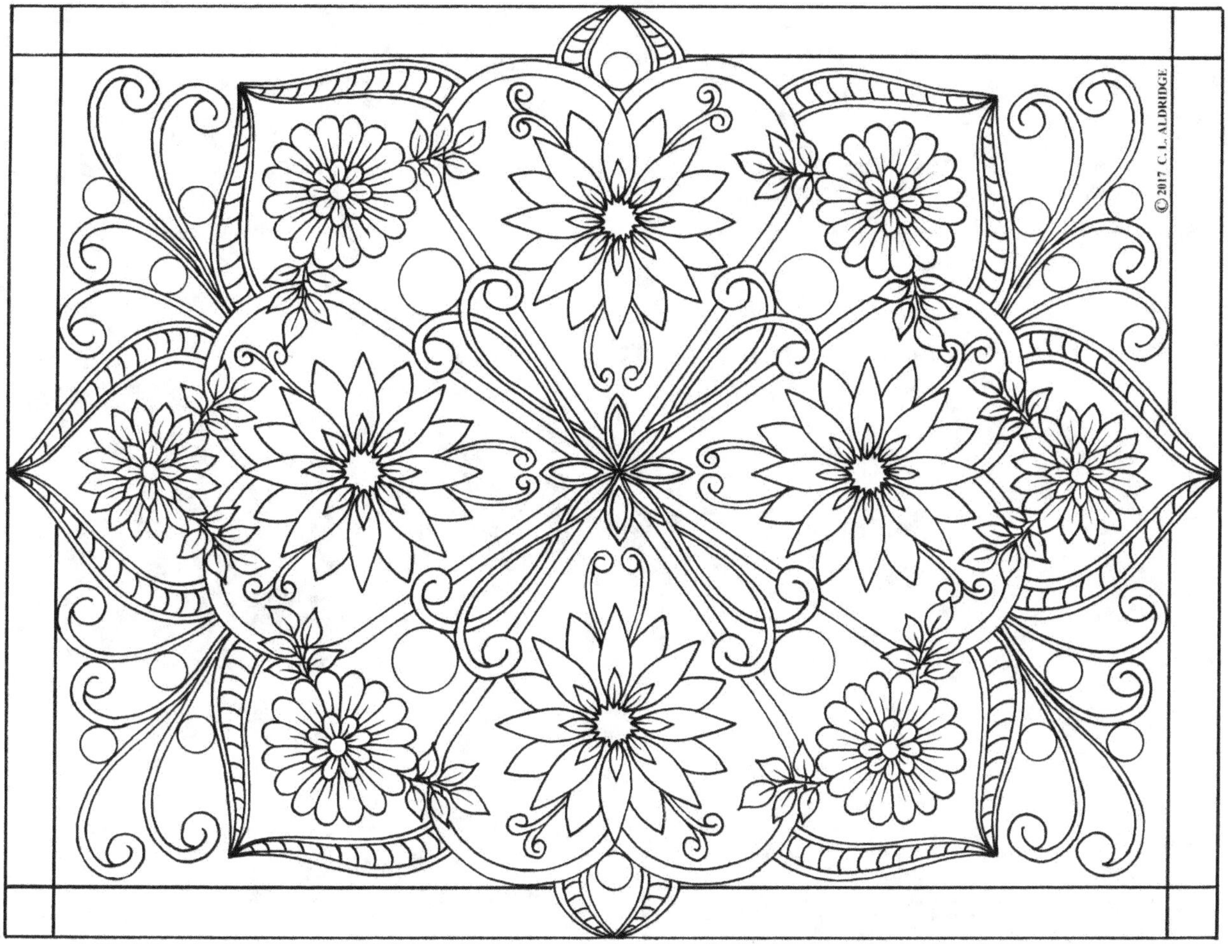

© 2017 C.L. Aldridge

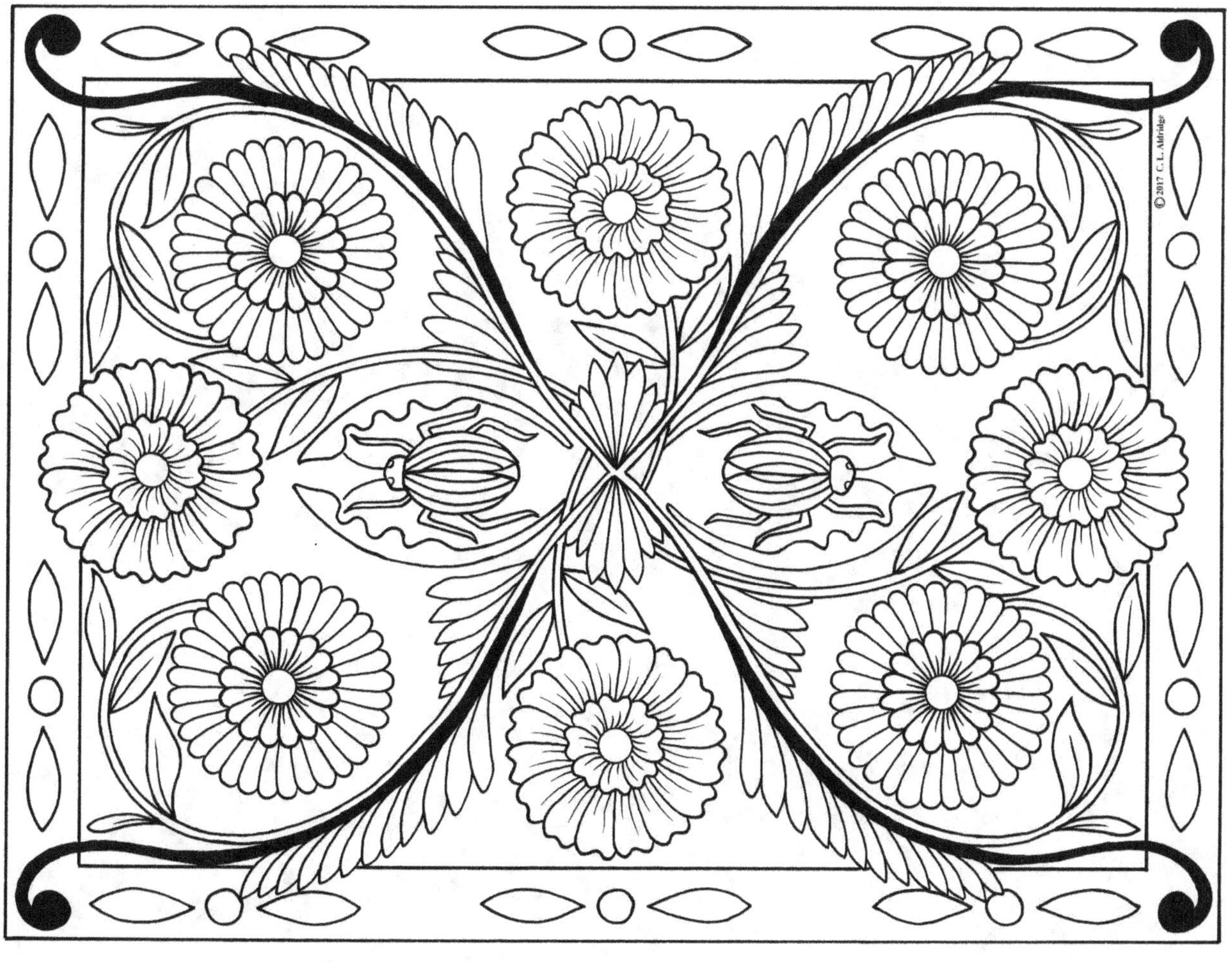

© 2017 C.L. Aldridge

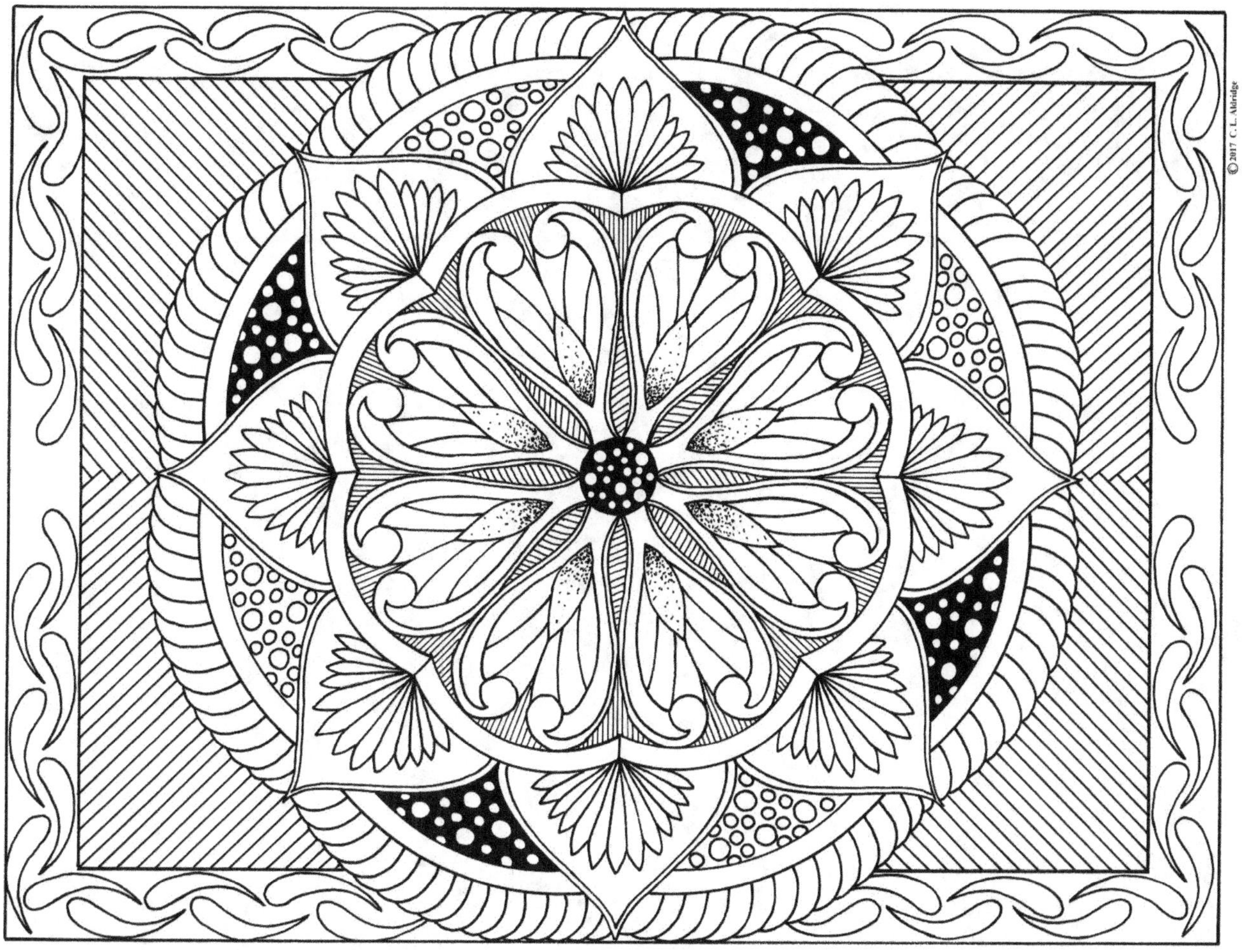
© 2017 C. L. Aldridge

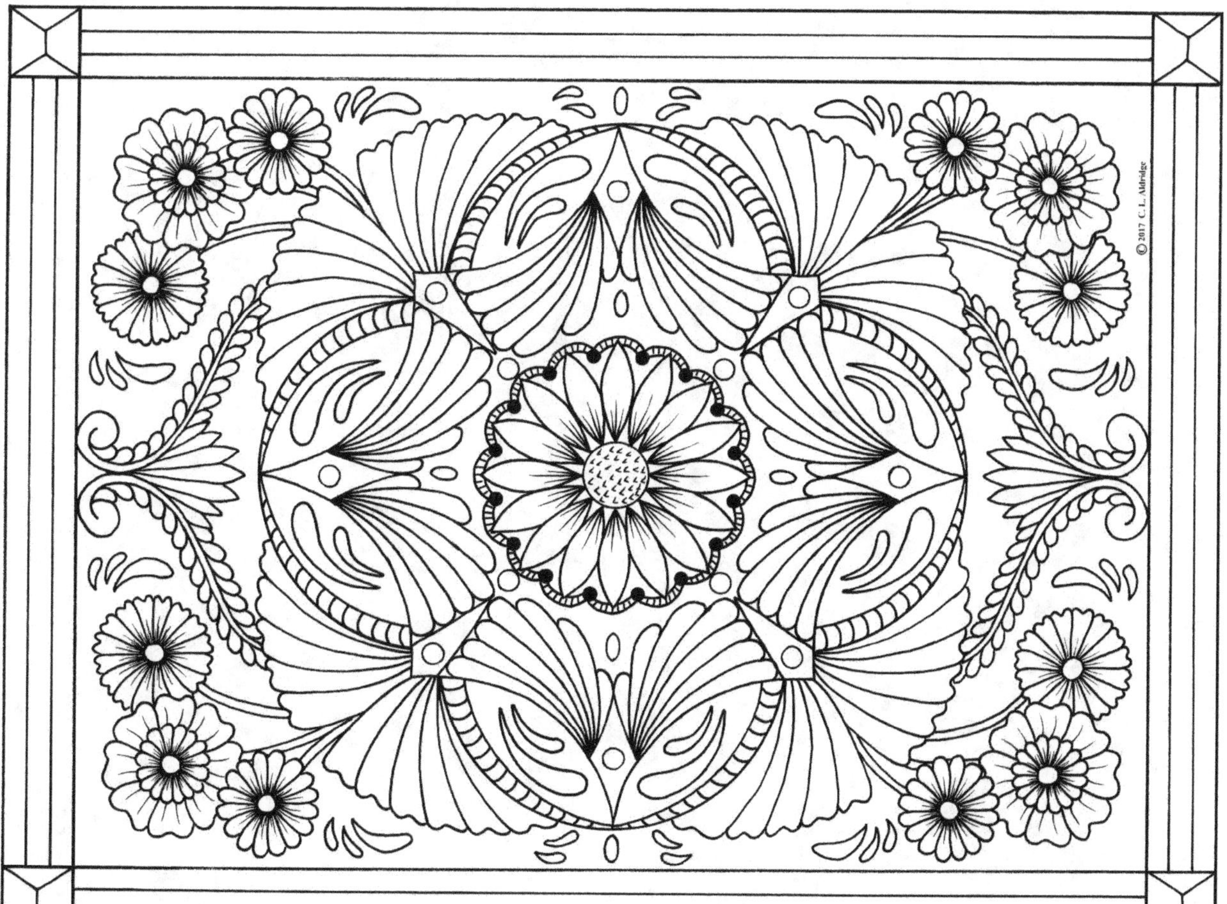
© 2017 C. L. Aldridge

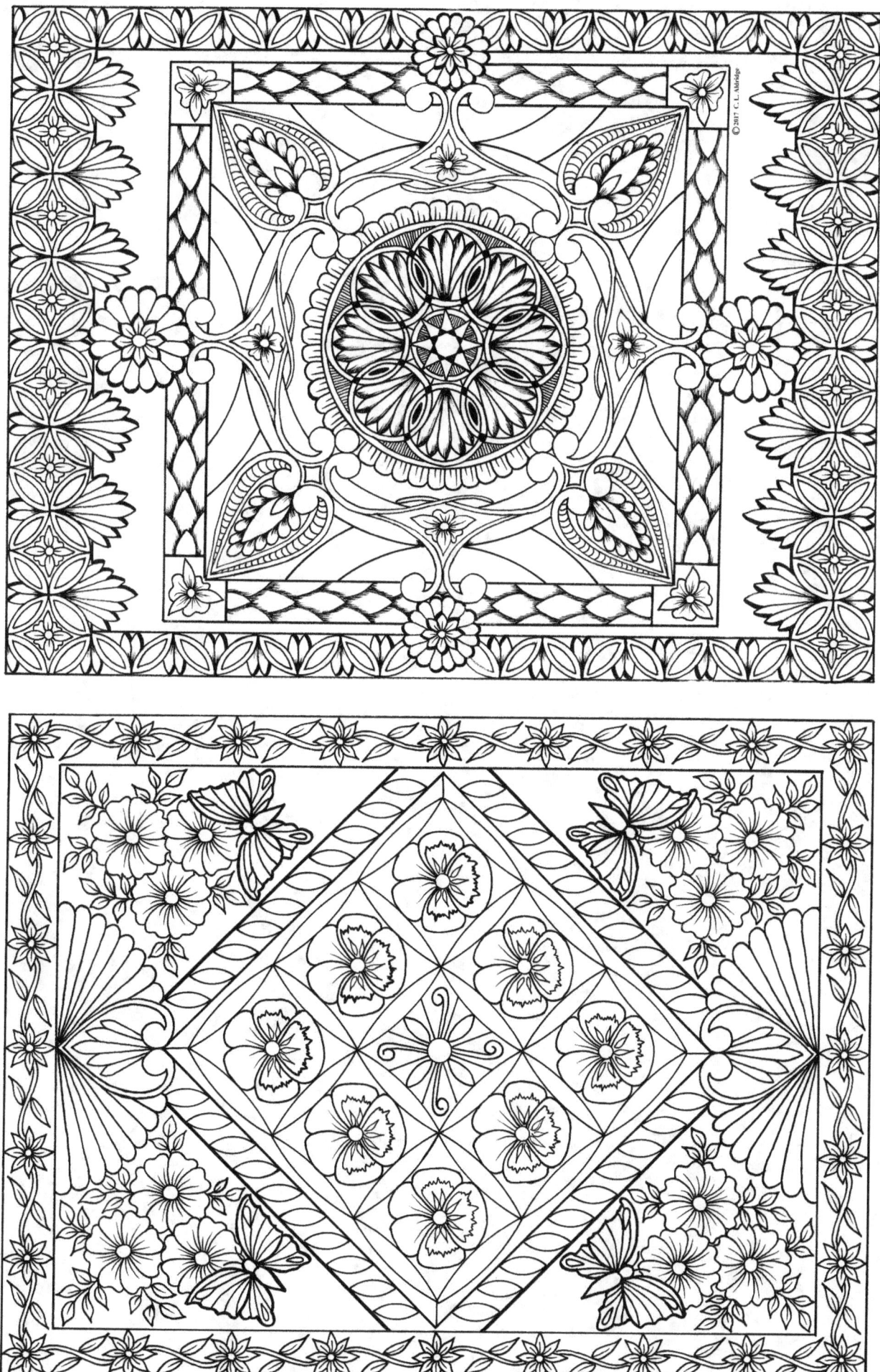

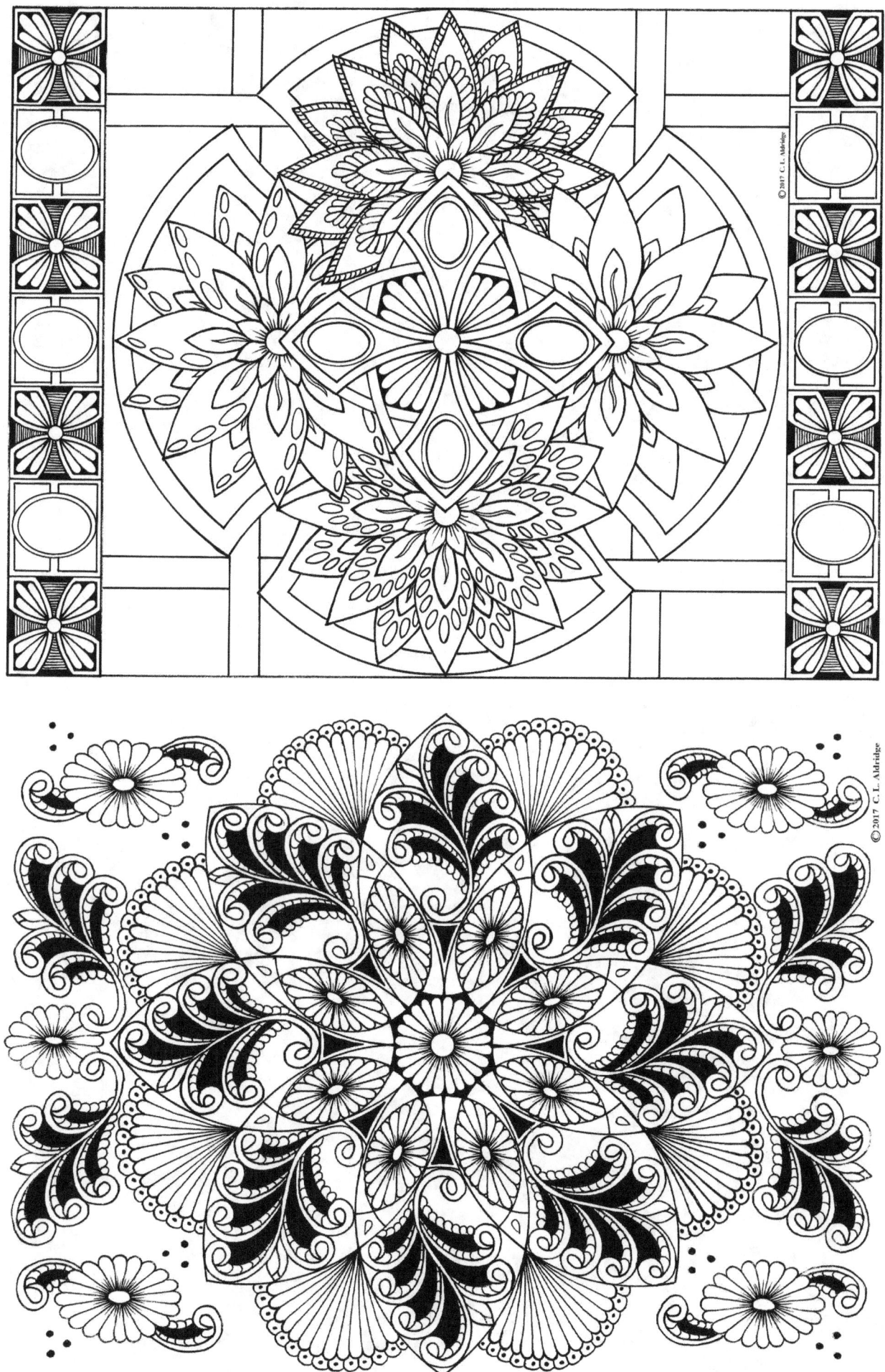

©2017 C.L.ALDRIDGE

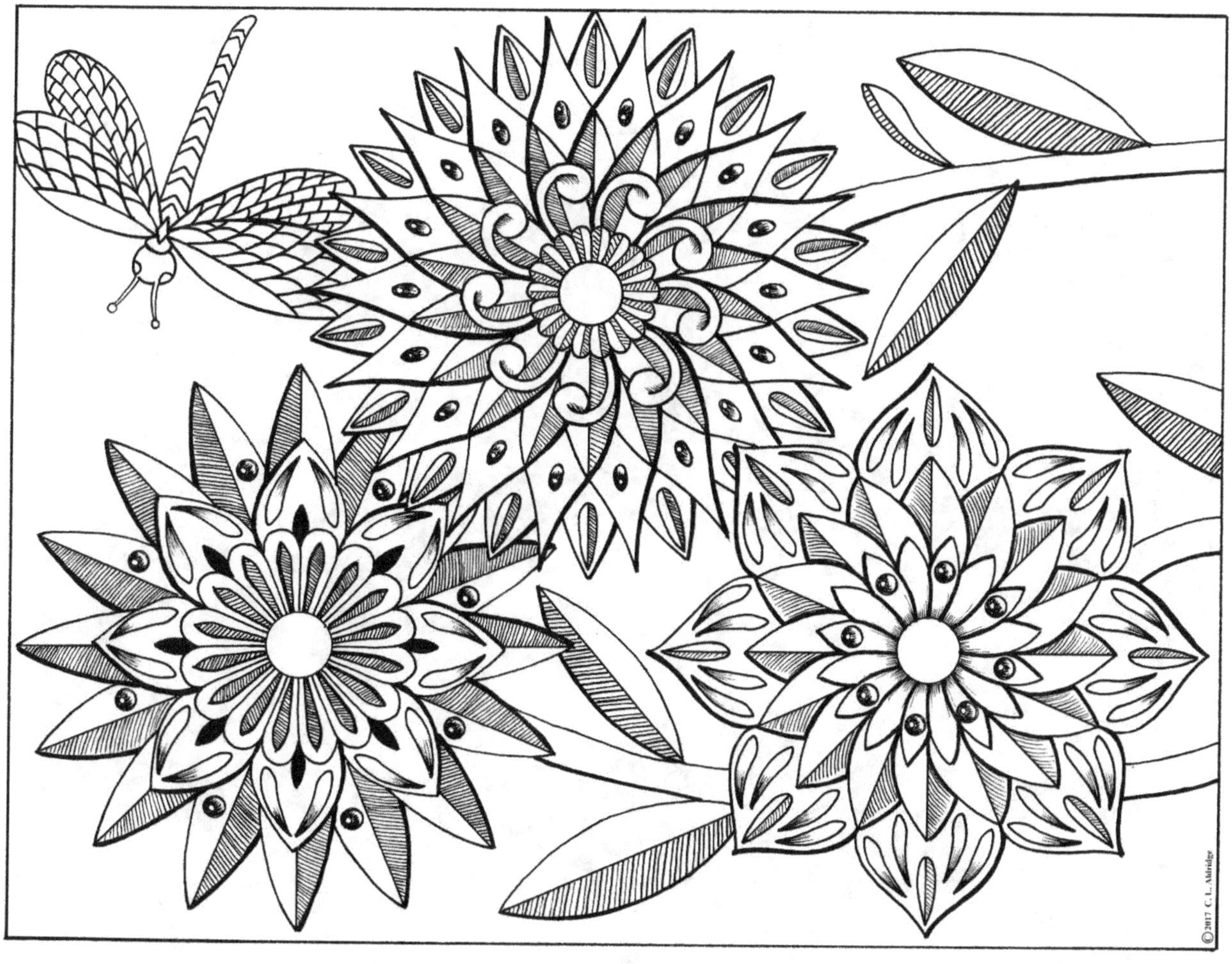
©2017 C.L. Aldridge

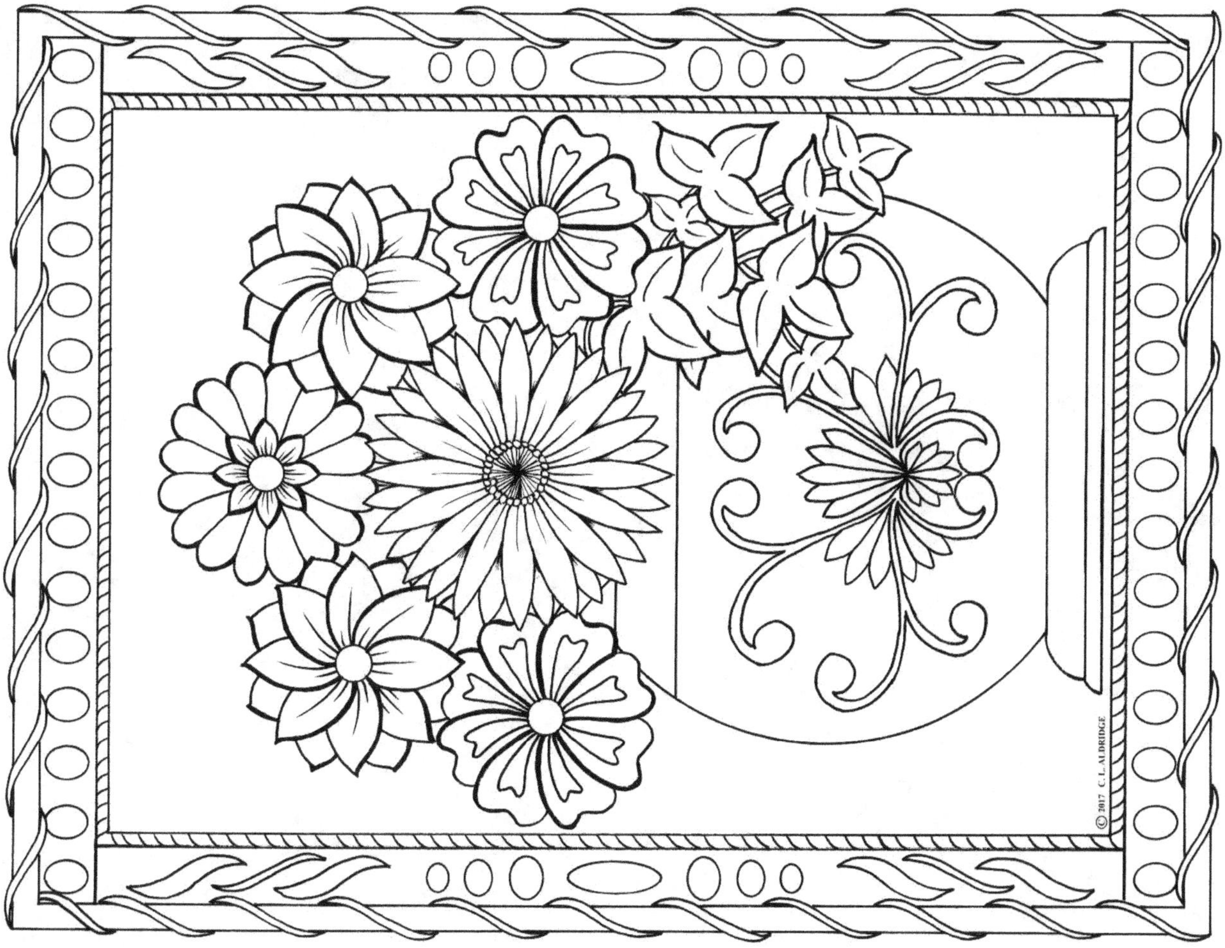

© 2017 C.L. ALDRIDGE

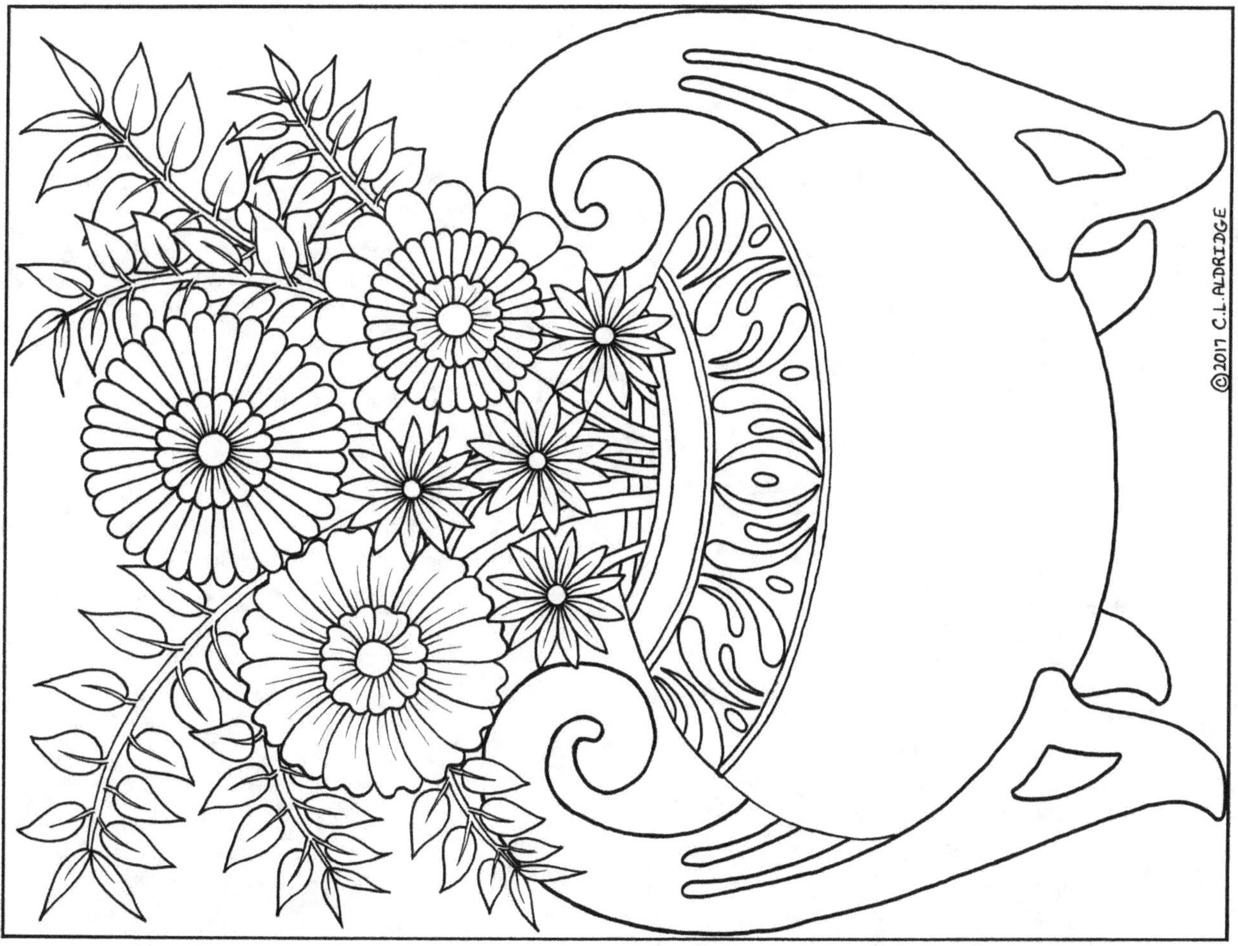

© 2017 C.L. ALDRIDGE

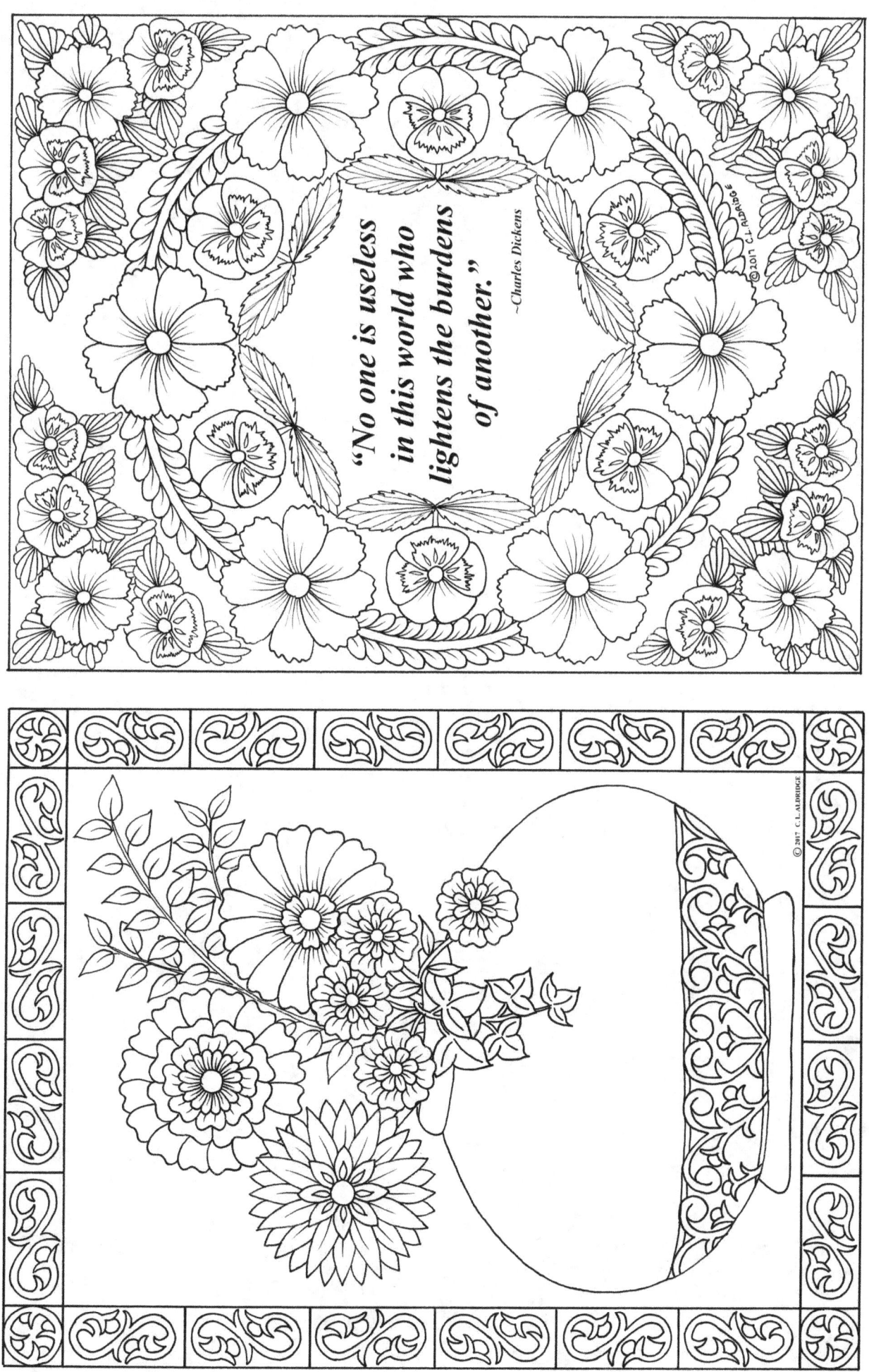

"No one is useless in this world who lightens the burdens of another."

~Charles Dickens

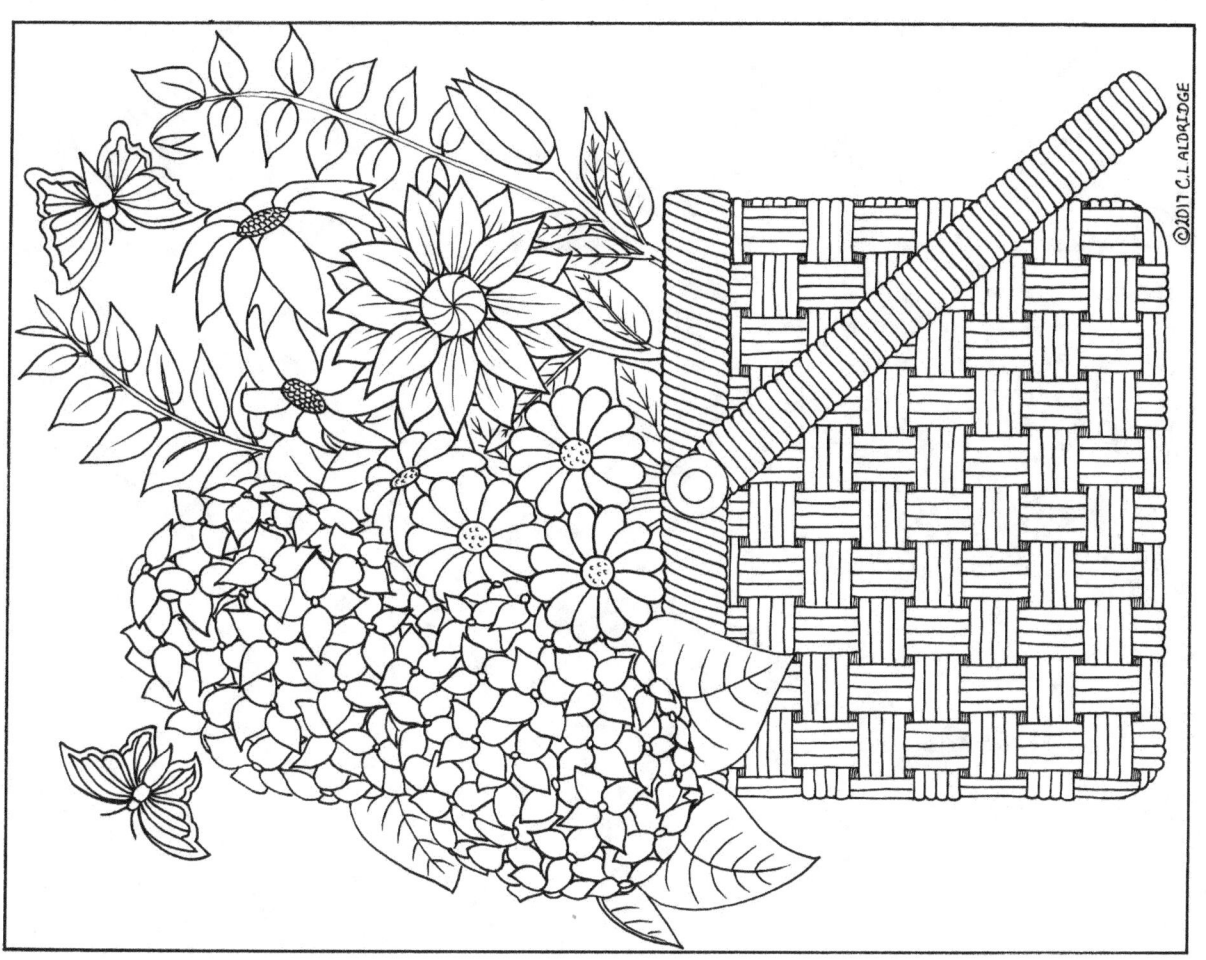

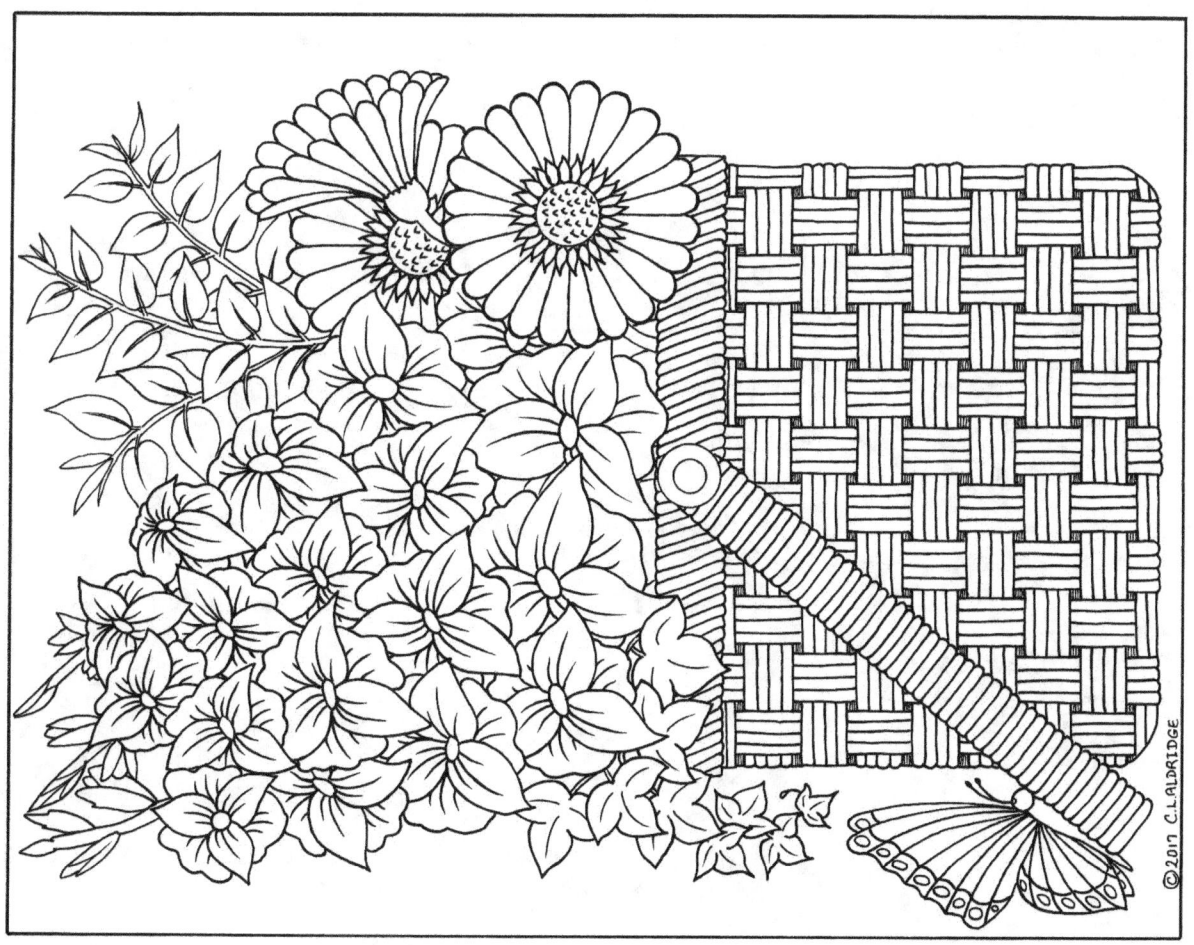

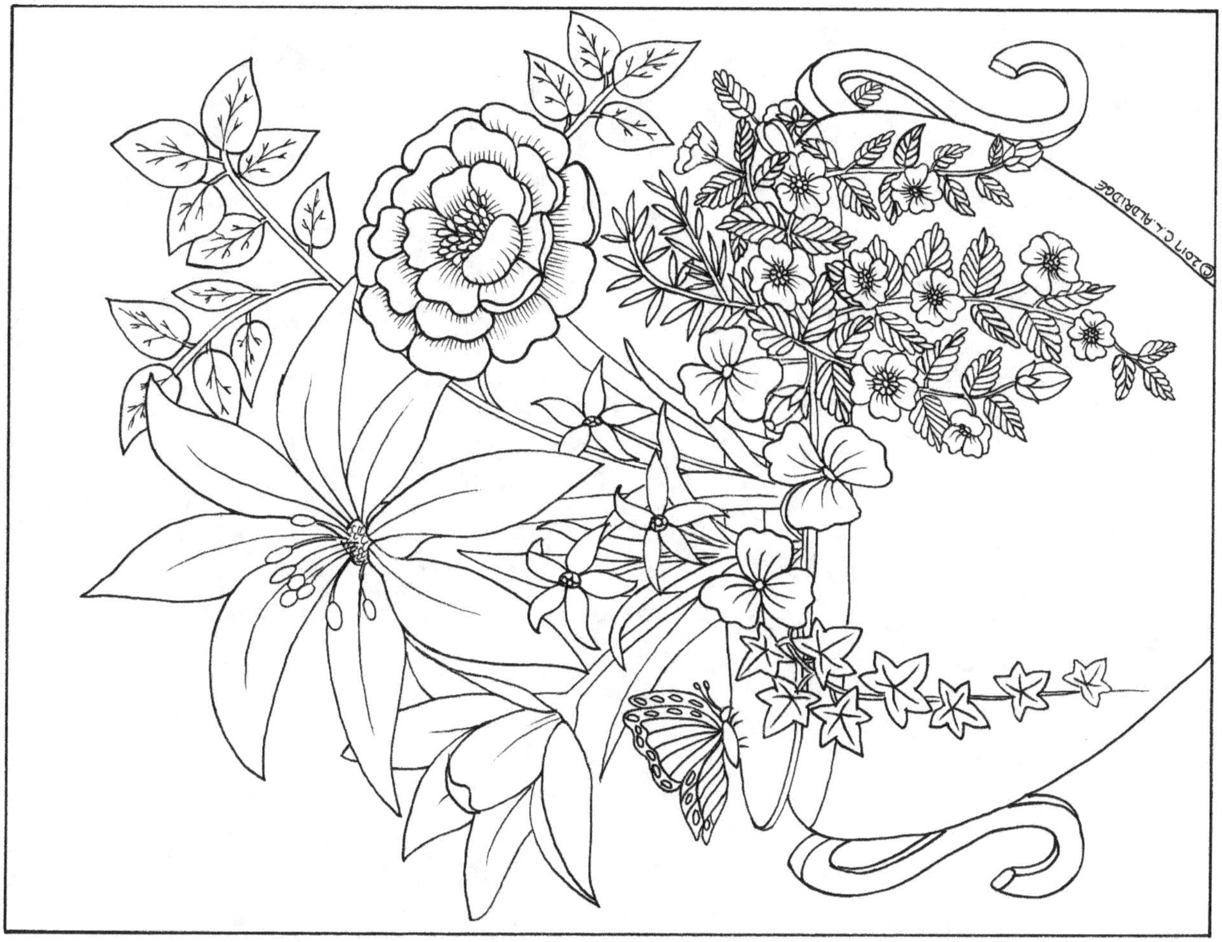
©2017 C.L.ALDRIDGE
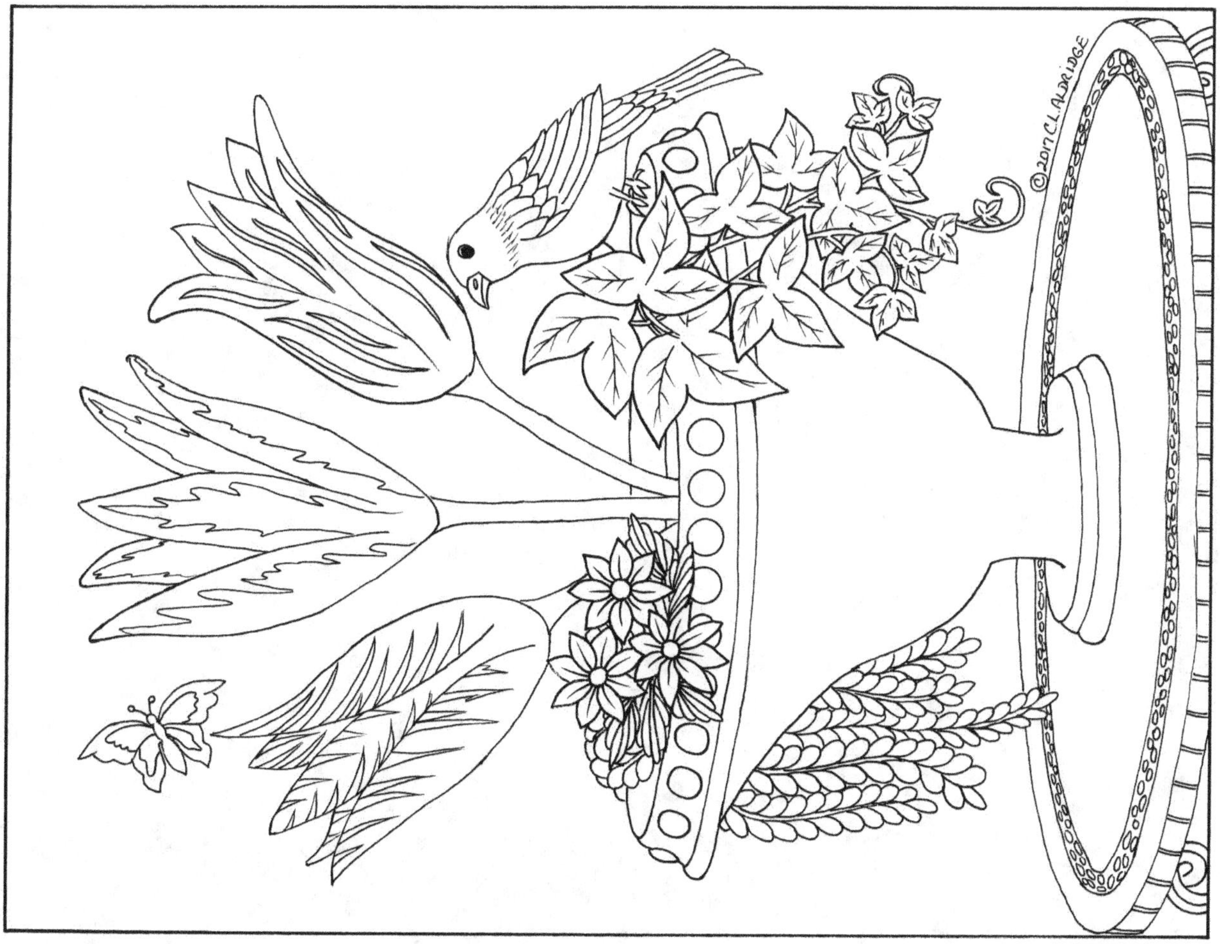
©2017 C.L.ALDRIDGE

Let me not to the marriage of true minds
Admit impediments. Love is not love
Which alters when it alteration finds,
Or bends with the remover to remove:
O no! it is an ever-fixed mark
That looks on tempests and is never shaken;

Sonnet 116 ~ William Shakespeare

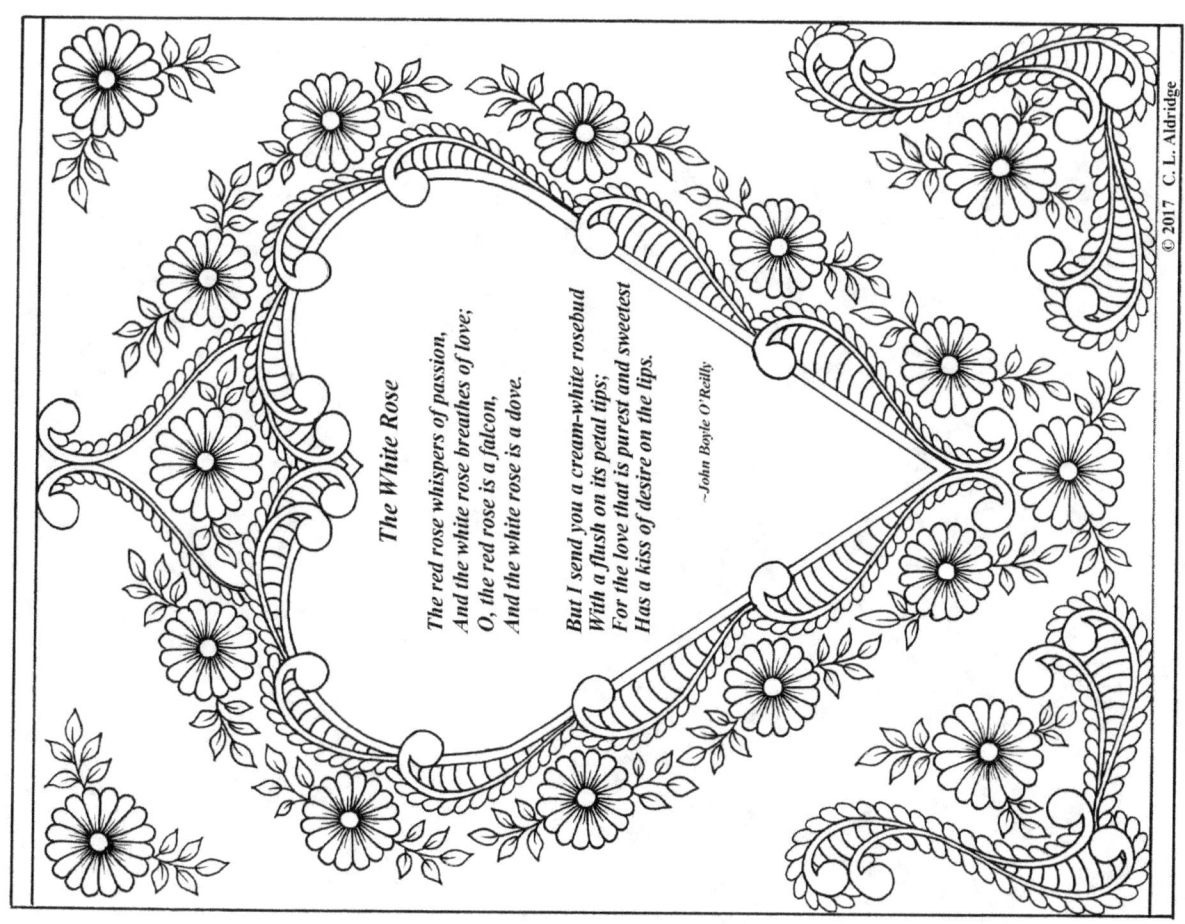

The White Rose

The red rose whispers of passion,
And the white rose breathes of love;
O, the red rose is a falcon,
And the white rose is a dove.

But I send you a cream-white rosebud
With a flush on its petal tips;
For the love that is purest and sweetest
Has a kiss of desire on the lips.

–John Boyle O'Reilly.

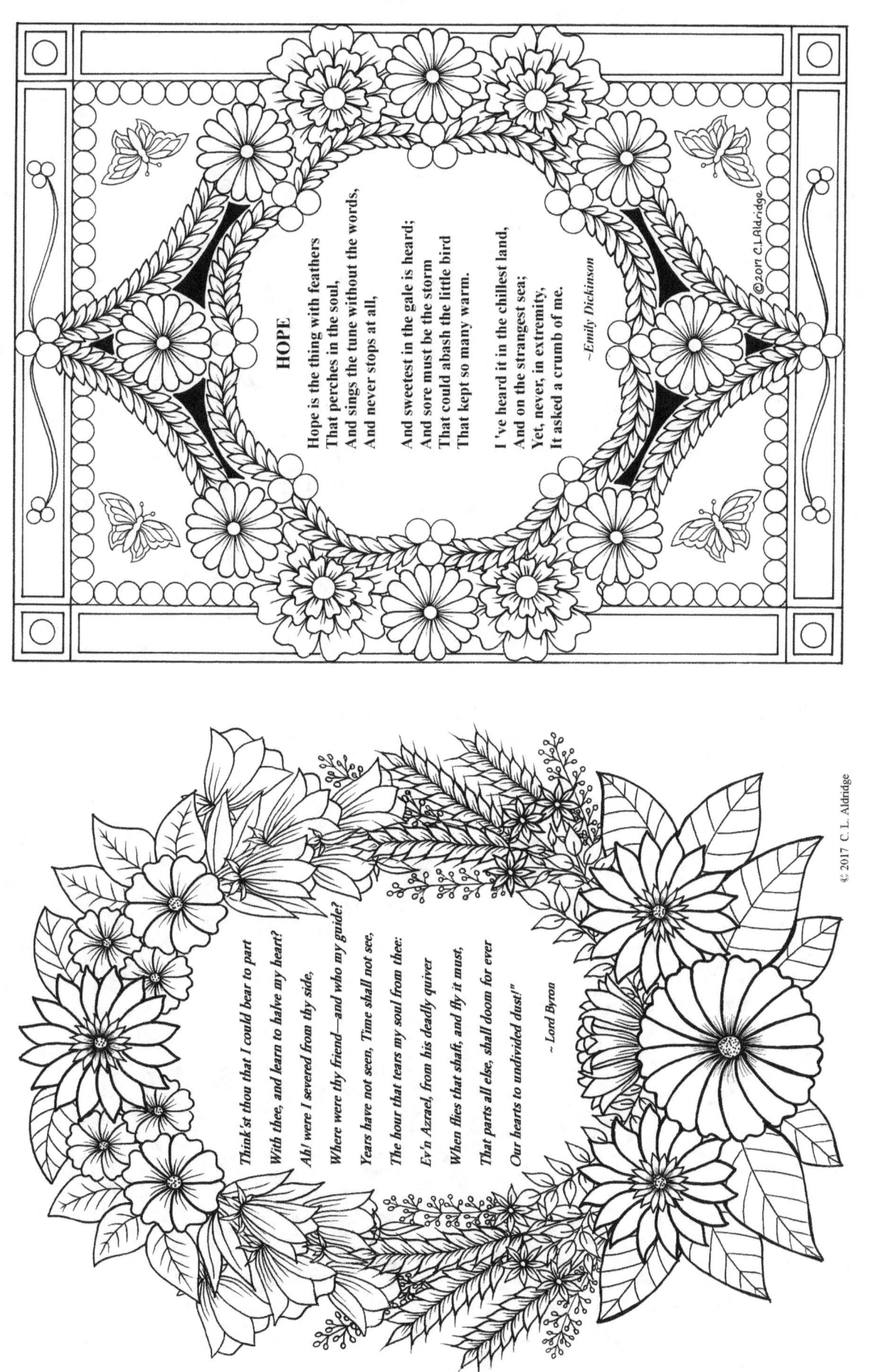

HOPE

Hope is the thing with feathers
That perches in the soul,
And sings the tune without the words,
And never stops at all,

And sweetest in the gale is heard;
And sore must be the storm
That could abash the little bird
That kept so many warm.

I've heard it in the chillest land,
And on the strangest sea;
Yet, never, in extremity,
It asked a crumb of me.

~Emily Dickinson

Think'st thou that I could bear to part
With thee, and learn to halve my heart?
Ah! were I severed from thy side,
Where were thy friend—and who my guide?
Years have not seen, Time shall not see,
The hour that tears my soul from thee:
Ev'n Azrael, from his deadly quiver
When flies that shaft, and fly it must,
That parts all else, shall doom for ever
Our hearts to undivided dust!"

~ Lord Byron

EVEN MORE BONUS PAGES!

Not long ago I had a fan who went treasure hunting in my picture archives and unearthed many drawings I had done long before I ever thought of creating coloring books for the print market. Though I argued that they were too ink heavy (lots of black ink), or too small (some were developed for greeting cards, etc.,), she encouraged me to at least offer them as PDF downloads from my Etsy shop at CLAldridgeArt. To my surprise they have been quite popular and have been beautifully colored and posted to Social Media several times.

Now I offer them to you to try out too!

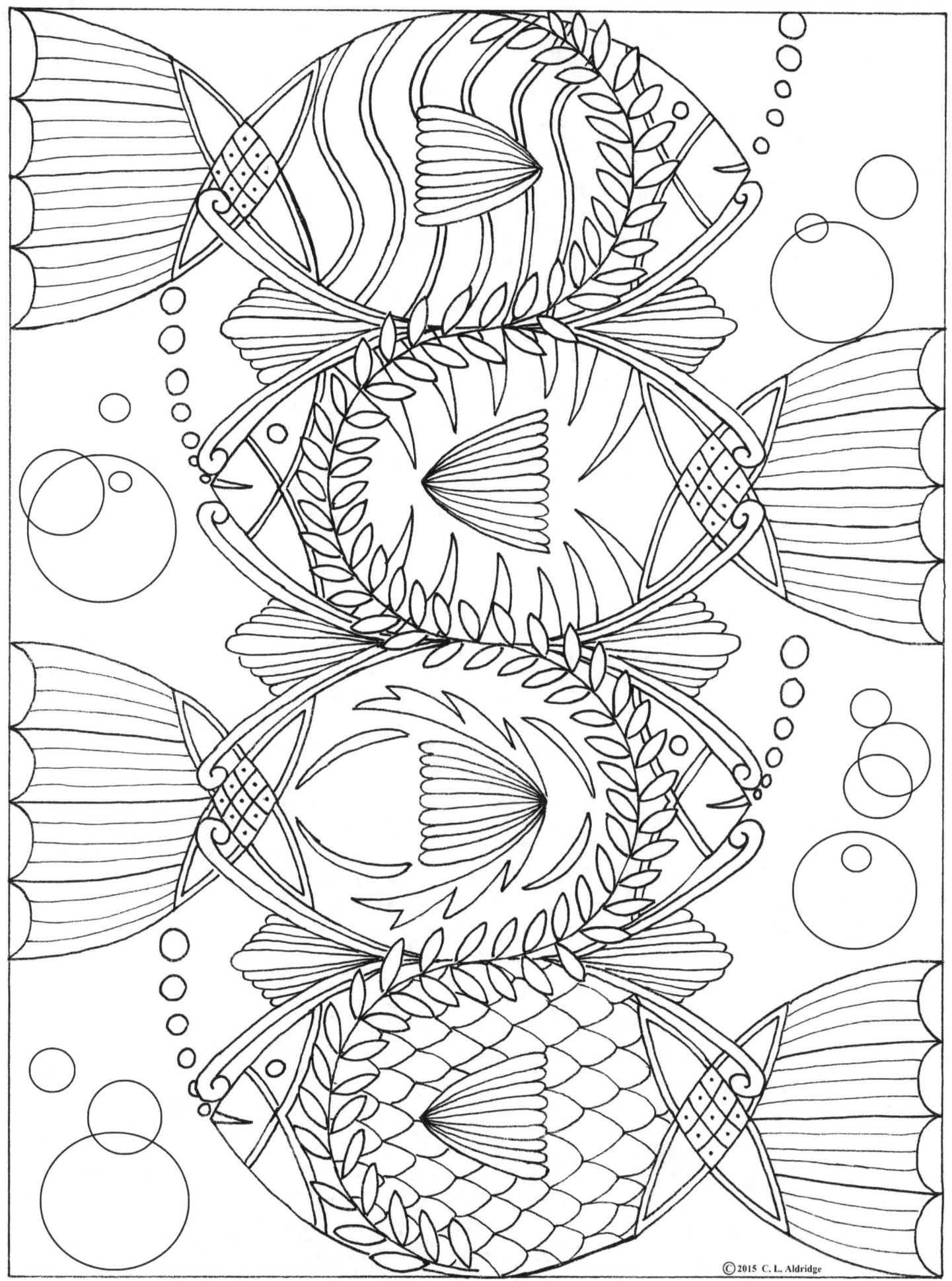

©2015 C. L. Aldridge

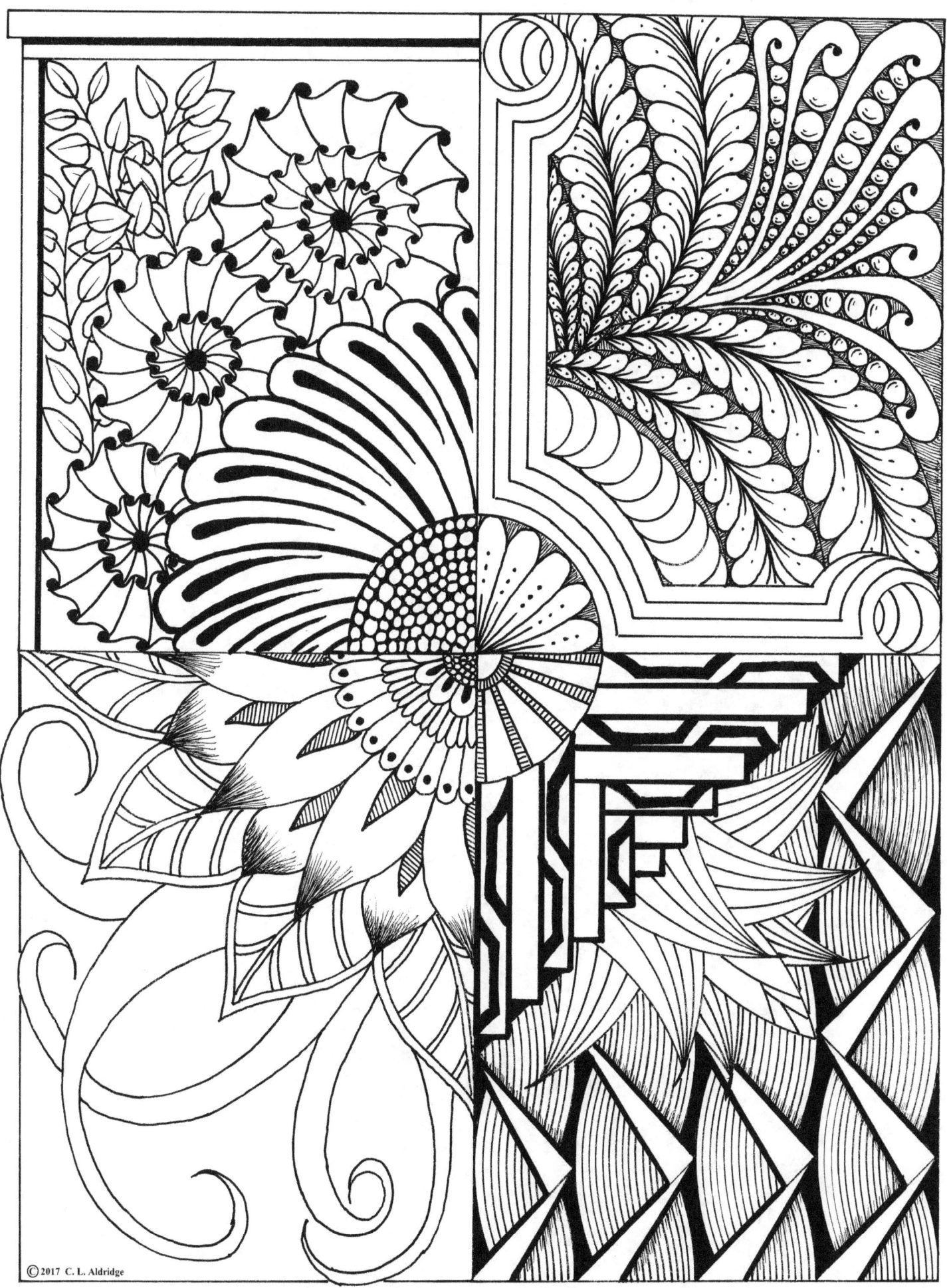

© 2017 C. L. Aldridge

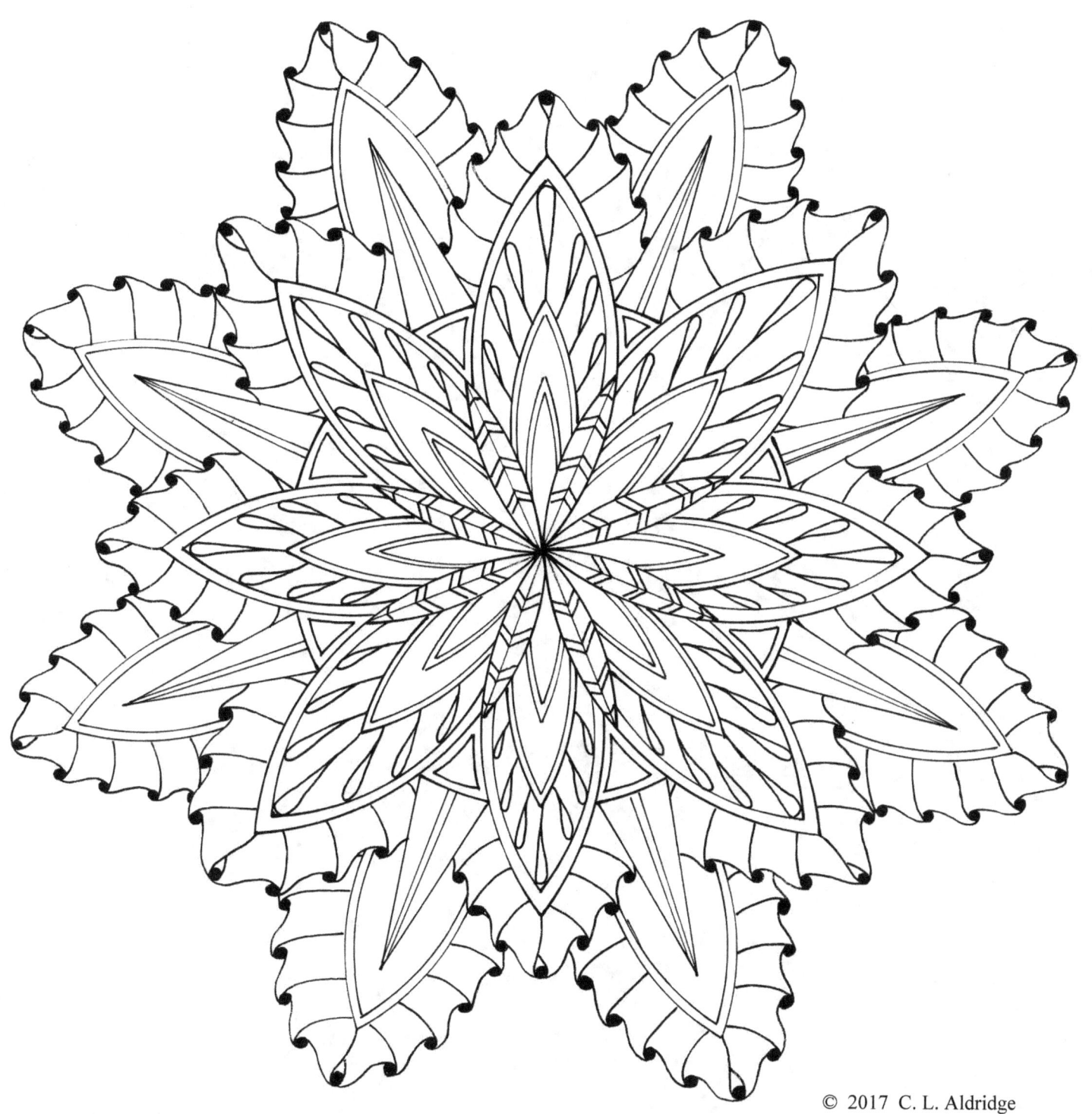

© 2017 C. L. Aldridge

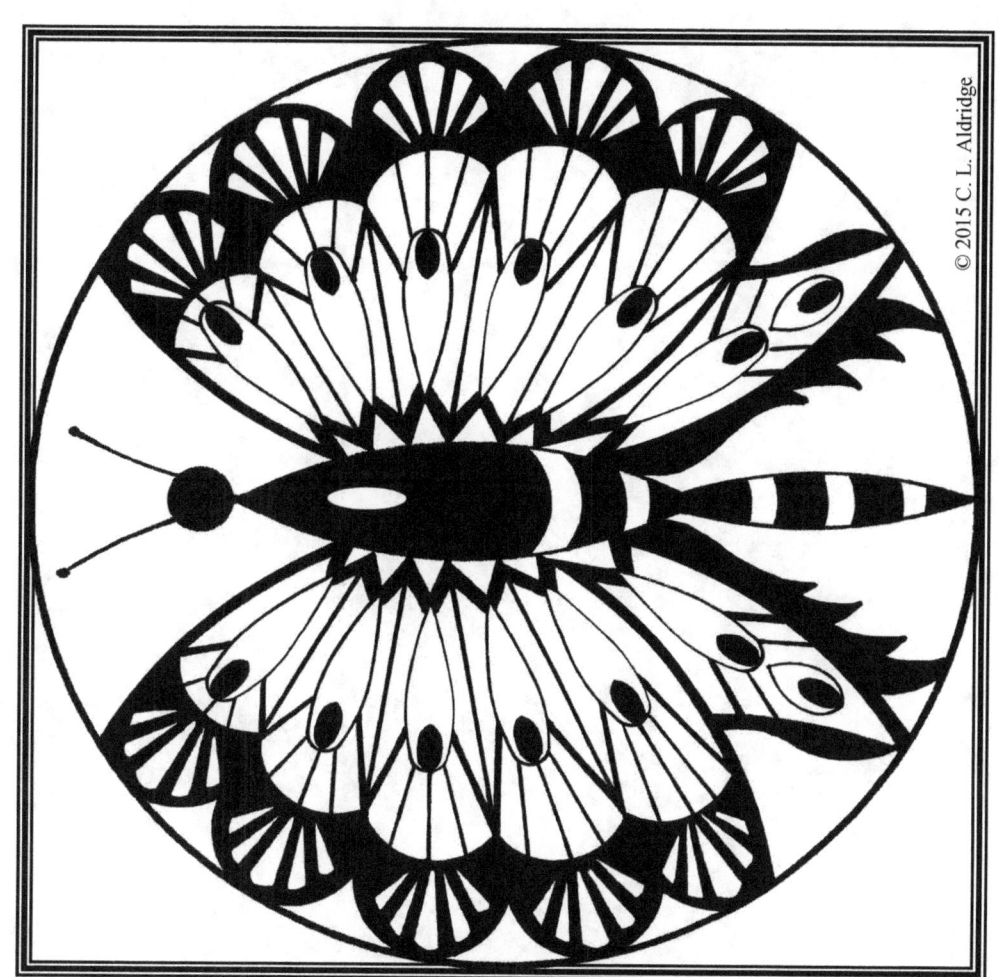

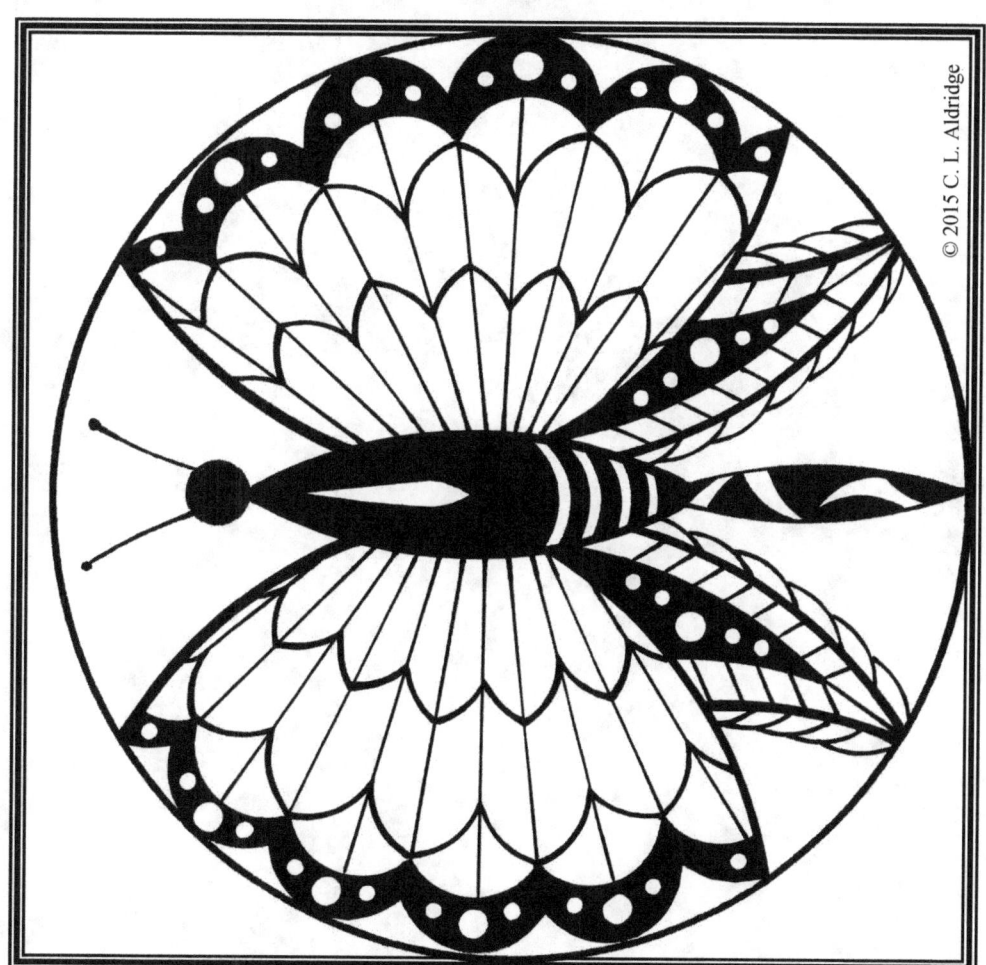

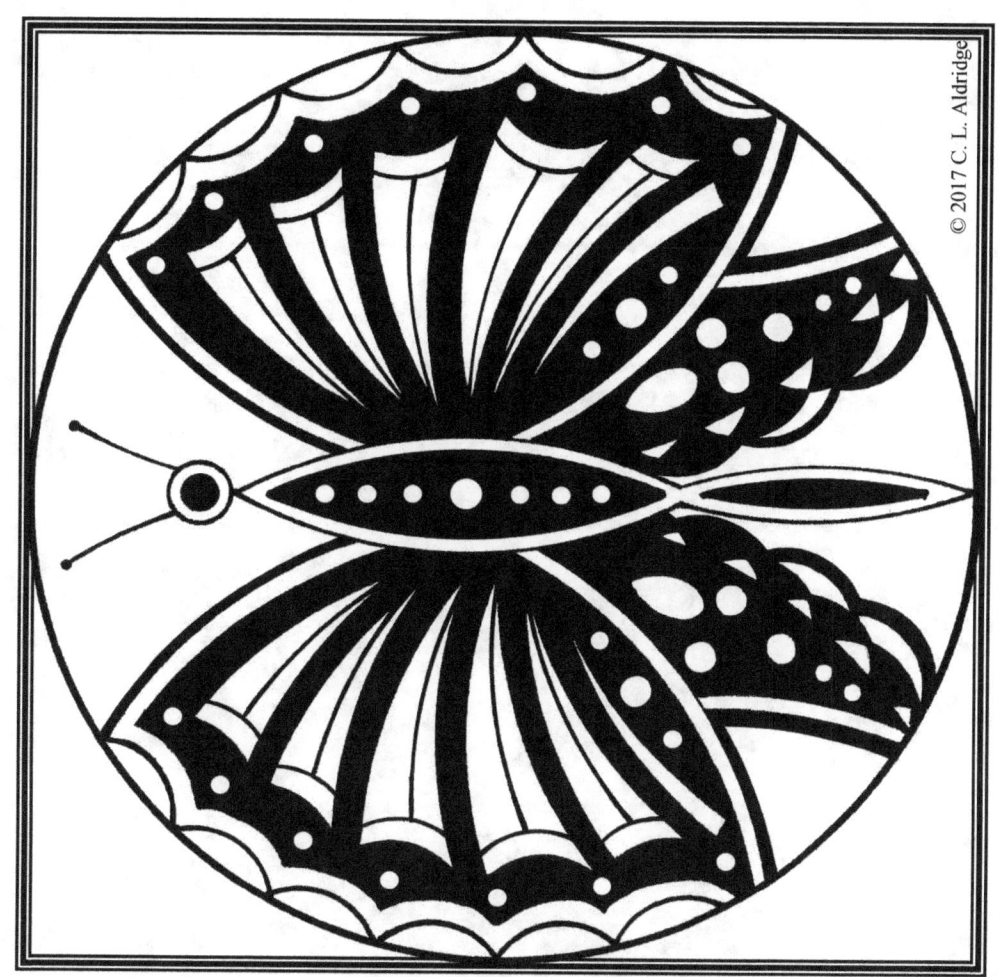

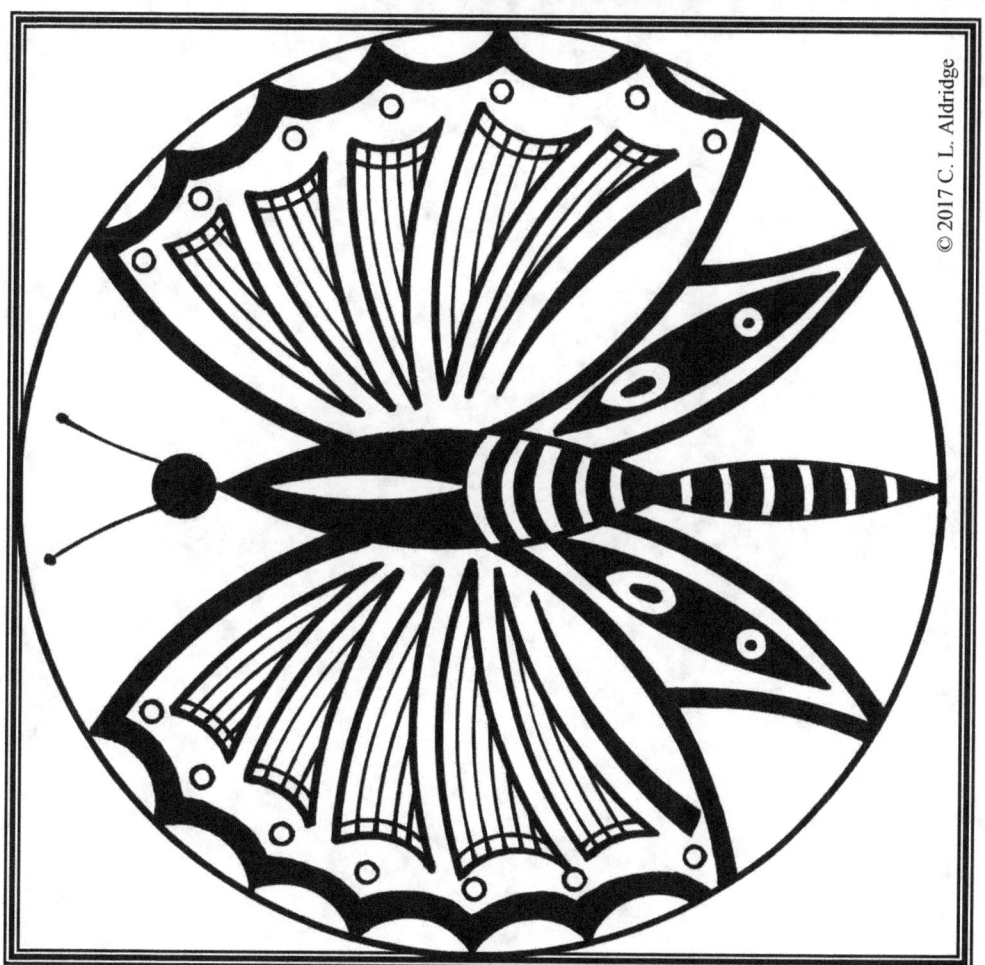

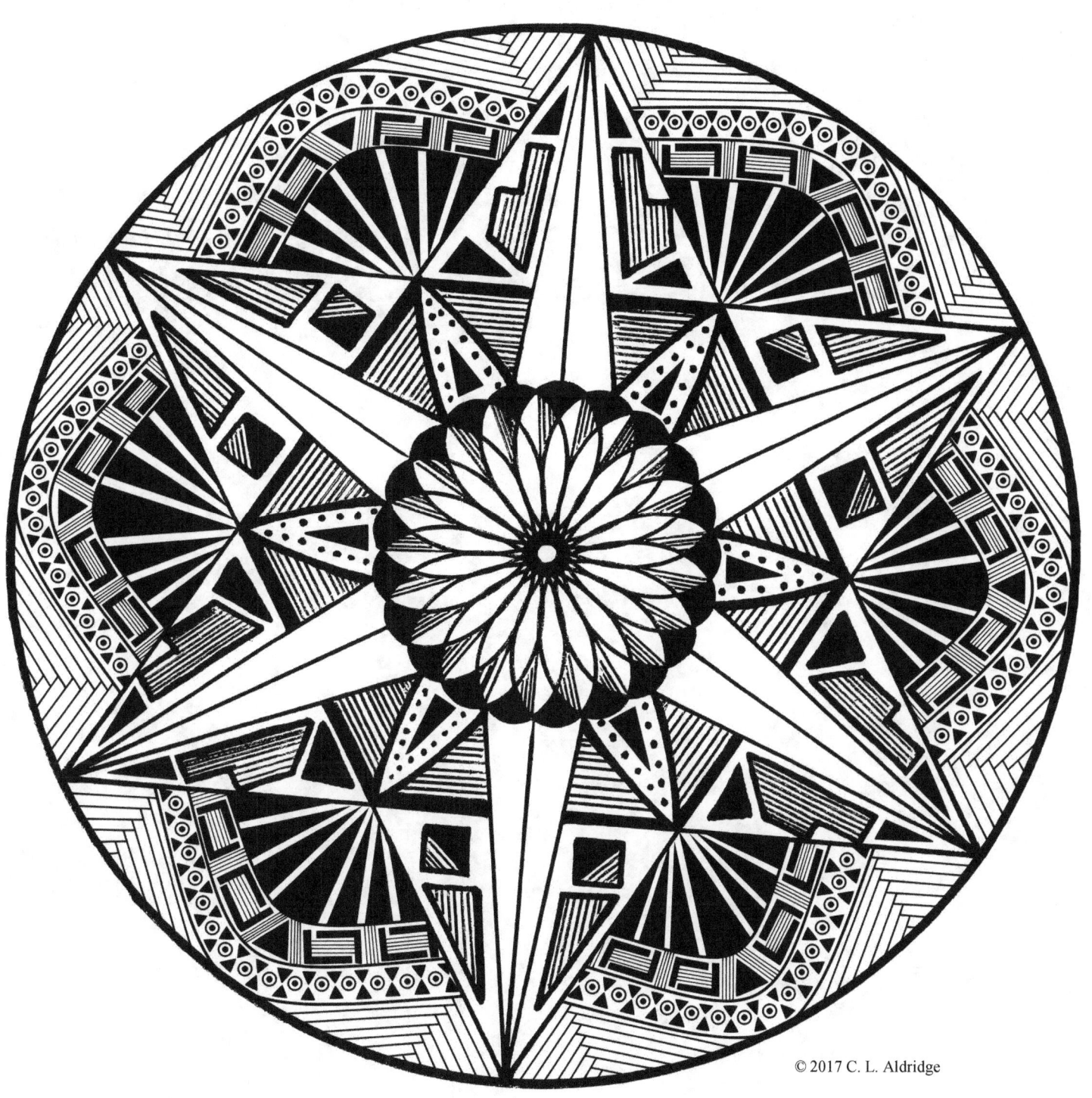

© 2017 C. L. Aldridge

This page has intentionally been left blank for use as either
a blotting page or color testing page.

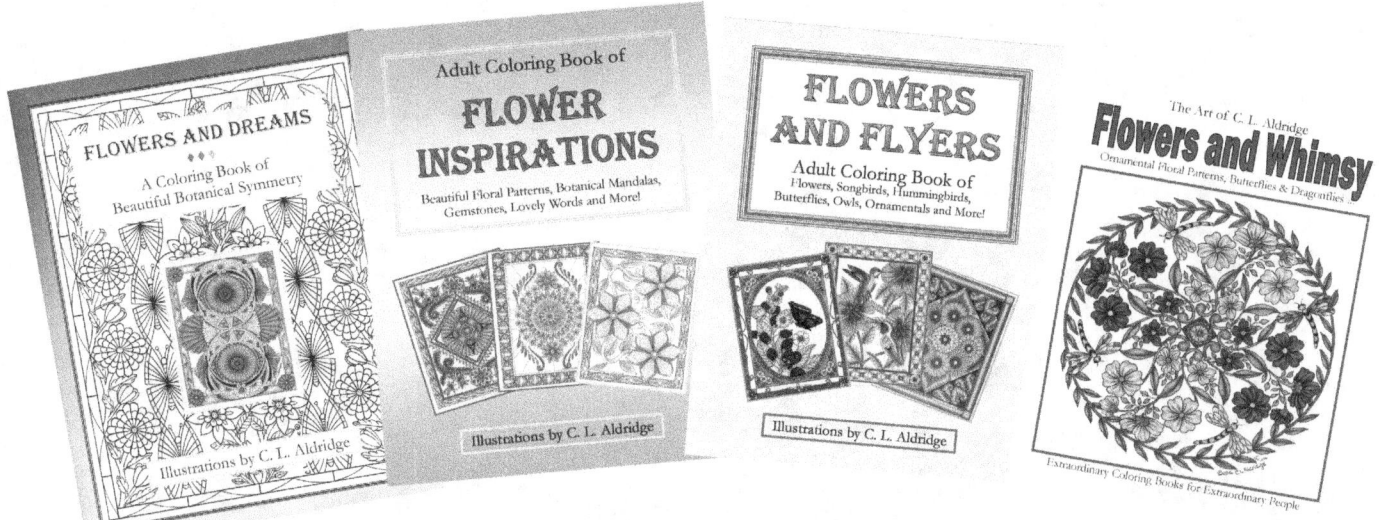

Extraordinary Coloring Books for Extraordinary People

Available in Print at Amazon.com Worldwide

Or as a PDF at CLAldridgeArt on Etsy

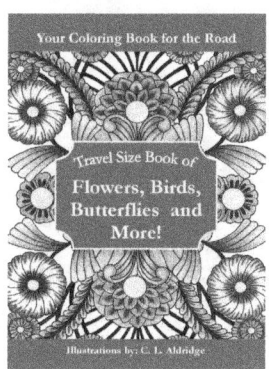

PLEASE COME JOIN US AT

C. L. Aldridge's, Coloring In Bloom—Coloring Club

On FACEBOOK. Post your beautiful colorings and be inspired by the coloring of other fans of C. L. Aldridge Art, we'll leave a light on for you!

If you like these books, please consider leaving your review on Amazon.com

www.ingramcontent.com/pod-product-compliance
Lightning Source LLC
Chambersburg PA
CBHW081201180526
45170CB00006B/2180